WRITING WITH EASE, REVISED EDITION

Level Three

part of *The Complete Writer*

INSTRUCTOR GUIDE

By

Susan Wise Bauer

and Susanna Jarrett

WELL-TRAINED MIND PRESS

18021 The Glebe Lane
Charles City, VA 23030
www.welltrainedmind.com

Names: Bauer, Susan Wise, author. | Jarrett, Susanna, author.
Title: Writing with ease. Level three, Instructor guide / by Susan Wise Bauer and Susanna Jarrett.
Description: Revised edition. | Charles City, VA : Well-Trained Mind Press, [2025] | Series: Complete writer. | For instructors of students ages 8 to 9.
Identifiers: ISBN: 9781944481599 (paperback)
Subjects: LCSH: English language--Rhetoric--Study and teaching (Elementary) | English language--Composition and exercises--Study and teaching (Elementary) | LCGFT: Teachers' guides. | BISAC: EDUCATION / Teaching / Subjects / Language Arts. | JUVENILE NONFICTION / Language Arts / Composition & Creative Writing.
Classification: LCC: LB1576 .B383 2025 | DDC: 372.62/3--dc23

1 2 3 4 5 6 7 8 9 10 Versa 30 29 28 27 26 25

Cover Design by Shane Klink

CONTENTS

READING SELECTIONS

Week 1: "The Straw, the Coal, and the Bean" and "Cat and Mouse in Partnership" by Jacob and Wilhelm Grimm

Week 2: *Mr. Revere and I* by Robert Lawson

Week 3: *And Then What Happened, Paul Revere?* by Jean Fritz and *The Many Rides of Paul Revere* by James Cross Giblin

Week 4: *Homer Price* by Robert McCloskey

Week 5: "Jabberwocky" by Lewis Carroll and "Stegosaurus" by Jack Prelutsky

Week 6: *Time Cat* by Lloyd Alexander

Week 7: *The Story of the World, Volume 1: Ancient Times* and *The Story of the World, Volume 2: The Middle Ages* by Susan Wise Bauer

Week 8: *The Lion, the Witch and the Wardrobe* by C. S. Lewis

Week 9: *C. S. Lewis: The Man Behind Narnia* by Beatrice Gormley and *Everyday Life: World War I* by Walter A. Hazen

Week 10: *Farmer Boy* by Laura Ingalls Wilder

Week 11: *Tales of Ancient Egypt* by Roger Lancelyn Green and *The Histories* by Herodotus, trans. by Robin Waterfield

Week 12: "Ali Baba and the Forty Thieves" by Jacob and Wilhelm Grimm

Week 13: *The Four-Story Mistake* by Elizabeth Enright

Week 14: *The Moffats* by Eleanor Estes

Week 15: *The Lemonade Trick* by Scott Corbett

Week 16: *Magic . . . Naturally! Science Entertainments and Amusements* by Vicki Cobb, and Adapted from *Magic Through Science* by Robert Gardner

Week 17: *Harry Houdini, Young Magician* by Kathryn Kilby Borland and *Harry Houdini: Death-Defying Showman* by Rita Thievon Mullin

Week 18: *Paul Bunyan Swings His Axe* by Dell J. McCormick and *The Story of Canada* by Janet Lunn and Christopher Moore

Week 19: *The Story of the Declaration of Independence* by Norman Richards and *The Young Oxford History of Britain & Ireland* by Mike Corbishley and Kenneth O. Morgan

Week 20: "The Garden of Live Flowers" and "Queen Alice" from *Through the Looking-Glass* by Lewis Carroll

Week 21: "Stopping by Woods on a Snowy Evening" by Robert Frost and "The Listeners" by Walter de la Mare

Week 22: *The Furious Flycycle* by Jan Wahl

Week 23: "Two Great Painters" from *Fifty Famous People: A Book of Short Stories*, by James Baldwin and "Samuel Finley Breese Morse" from *The Child's Book of American Biography*, by Mary Stoyell Stimpson

Week 24: *Mrs. Piggle-Wiggle's Magic* by Betty MacDonald

Week 25: *Money, Money, Money: Where It Comes From, How to Save It, Spend It, and Make It* by Eve Drobot and *The Everything Kids' Money Book* by Diane Mayr

Week 26: *Babe: The Gallant Pig* by Dick King-Smith

Week 27: *Hunting and Herding Dogs* by Marie-Therese Miller and *A Dog's World,* edited by Christine Hunsicker

Week 28: *Anne of Green Gables* by Lucy Maud Montgomery and *Pioneers in Canada* by Harry Johnston

Week 29: *Young Folks' History of England* by Charlotte Yonge

Week 30: *The Black Stallion* by Walter Farley

Week 31: *King Arthur and His Knights of the Round Table* by Roger Lancelyn Green

Week 32: "The Valiant Little Tailor" by Jacob and Wilhelm Grimm

Week 33: *Bambi: A Life in the Woods* by Felix Salten

Week 34: "Prince Wicked and the Grateful Animals" from More *More Jataka Tales* by Ellen Babbitt

Week 35: *The Jungle Book* by Rudyard Kipling

Week 36: *Rabbit Hill* by Robert Lawson

NOTE TO THE REVISED EDITION: HOW TO USE THE NEW CREATIVE WRITING LESSONS

At the end of each week, there is a bonus lesson. These lessons provide prompts to spark a young writer's imagination. They will satisfy the needs of students who could benefit from a creative writing outlet, while reinforcing concepts and skills students have practiced throughout the week.

These lessons are completely optional! If you skipped each one, your child would not be behind. The first four assignments each week cover everything students need to develop their writing skills.

In this second edition, we want to account for the fact that children think and learn in different ways. At this age, some students are not ready for creative writing, and there is nothing to be gained in forcing them to do it. Meanwhile, other students crave opportunities to practice their new skills in a creative way. You know your child best, and can decide whether or not your student will benefit from this extra practice.

If you decide to use the bonus lessons, be sure to read these parameters first:

The creative writing lessons typically consist of a single writing prompt (exceptions are noted within the lessons). Some students will be able to write their answers to the prompt without additional help. If your student wants to complete the exercise but still struggles to get words down on paper, follow these three steps:

1. **Verbal Narration:** Read the prompt and have your student narrate her answer to you.
2. **Model Sentence:** Write down the first sentence of their narration (modifying when necessary to simplify or shorten).
3. **Dictation:** (1) read the student's sentence back to her and (2) have her repeat it back to you. (3) Have her write the sentence down on her own, without access to the written model. Repeat steps 1-2 if necessary until the student has written the full sentence.

The prompts in these lessons are designed to awaken a student's creativity. After completing the first sentence, some students may want to draw a picture or write additional sentences on their own. Encourage this, but do not require it. While the first sentence should be checked and edited for grammar and spelling, do not require students to correct or edit any additional writing. Just encourage them!

WEEK 1

DAY ONE: Narration Exercise *Student Workbook pages 1–3*

***Focus:** Identifying the central narrative thread in a passage*

Pull out Student Workbook pages 1–2 and Student Workbook page 3. Ask the student to write her name and the date on Student Workbook page 3.

Allow the student to read the story on Student Workbook pages 1–2, either silently or aloud.

This fable is a more difficult narrative than the Level Two narratives. Help the student begin to identify the central elements in the narrative by asking the following questions. She should try to answer these questions without looking back at the story, but if she cannot remember an answer after thinking for a few minutes, allow her to reread. Remind her to answer in complete sentences.

Instructor: How did the bean escape from the old woman?
***Student:** It dropped out of the pan.*

Instructor: How did the coal escape from the fire?
***Student:** It leaped out.*

Instructor: What else escaped the fire?
***Student:** The straw escaped.*

Instructor: What did the bean, the coal, and the straw decide to do together?
***Student:** They decided to go on a journey to a foreign country.*

Instructor: What was the first obstacle they ran into?
***Student:** They came to a brook with no bridge across it.*

Instructor: What solution did the straw come up with?
***Student:** The straw laid herself across the water.*

Instructor: Who tried to cross the straw?
***Student:** The coal tried to cross.*

Instructor: What happened then?
***Student:** The coal burned through the straw and fell into the water.*

Instructor: How did the bean react?
***Student:** She laughed until she split.*

Instructor: Who fixed her?
***Student:** A tailor sewed her back together.*

> **Instructor:** This fairy tale is a particular kind of story called a "pourquoi [por-kwa] tale." *Pourquoi* is French for "why," and pourquoi tales give imaginative explanations for *why* something is the way it is. What does this tale try to explain?
> **Student:** *It tries to explain why beans have a black seam.*

Now ask the student the general question, "Can you give me a brief summary of this passage?" The student should answer by summarizing the plot, rather than listing details. Her answer should be no more than three sentences and should resemble one of the following:

> "A coal, a straw, and a bean escaped from an old woman. They set out on a journey, but the straw was burnt, the coal fell into water, and the bean split herself laughing. A tailor sewed up the bean with black thread."
>
> "A coal, a straw, and a bean set out on a journey. When they got to a brook, the straw lay down across it as a bridge. The coal went across the straw, but the straw burned, the coal fell into the water, and the bean burst herself laughing."
>
> "A coal, a straw, and a bean came to a brook. The straw tried to become a bridge, but the coal burned the bridge in half and fell in the water. Then the bean split open laughing."

The student will probably attempt to put too much information into the summary. If she has difficulty condensing the story, ask the following three questions:

> Who are the three main characters?
>
> What problem did they run into? ["They escaped from an old woman" **OR** "They came to a brook they could not cross" are both acceptable answers.]
>
> What happened to each one?

Then have the student repeat her answers in order; this will form her brief summary. Write down the student's narration on Student Workbook page 3 as she watches. When done, set the workbook page aside for the next lesson, which is on the back of it.

Day Two: Dictation Exercise *Student Workbook page 4*

***Focus:** Comma use, capitalization of proper names*

Pull out Student Workbook page 4. Ask the student to write her name and the date.

Tell the student that today's dictation sentence is from another one of the Grimms' fairy tales, called "Little Red Cap." It is one of the earliest versions of the story we now know as "Little Red Riding Hood."

Dictate the following sentence to the student two times. Before you read, tell the student that you will pause at the commas. Be sure to indicate the commas in the sentence by pausing significantly at each one.

> The grandmother lived out in the wood, half a mile from the village, and just as Little Red Cap entered the wood, a wolf met her.

Tell the student that since "Little Red Cap" is used as the girl's proper name, all three words should be capitalized. Now ask the student to repeat the sentence back to you before she writes. Remind her to pause, as you did, to indicate the commas. If she cannot remember the entire sentence, you may repeat it additional times.

Watch the student as she writes, and correct her at once if she begins to make a mistake. When she is finished, point out each comma and tell her that these commas are used to avoid misunderstanding. Without the commas, a reader might think that the grandmother lived in a "wood half a mile," or that Little Red Cap "entered the wood a wolf."

DAY THREE: Narration and Dictation — *Student Workbook pages 5–7*

***Focus:** Identifying the central narrative thread in a passage and writing original sentences from dictation*

Pull out Student Workbook pages 5–6 and 7. Ask the student to write her name and the date on Student Workbook page 7.

Today's exercise will combine narration and dictation. Allow the student to read the story on Student Workbook pages 5–6, either silently or aloud.

If the student is not familiar with the custom of "christening," you may want to explain that this is a church ceremony during which babies are baptized and named.

Help the student begin to identify the central elements in the narrative by asking the following questions. She should try to answer these questions without looking back at the story, but if she cannot remember an answer after thinking for a few minutes, allow her to reread. Remind her to answer in complete sentences.

Instructor: What did the cat and the mouse buy for the winter?
Student: *They bought a pot of bacon fat.*

Instructor: Where did they decide to keep it?
Student: *They kept it in the church.*

Instructor: What excuse did the cat give for going out and eating the fat?
Student: *She said that she had to go to christenings.*

Instructor: How many times did she do this?
Student: *She did it three times.*

Instructor: She told the mouse that the three babies had three strange names. What were they?
Student: *The names were Top-off, Half-done, and All-gone.*

Instructor: When the mouse found out what the cat had done, what happened?
Student: *The cat ate the mouse.*

Instructor: "That is the way of the world" means that the strong will always take advantage of the weak. In what two ways did the cat take advantage of the mouse?
Student: *She ate the bacon fat that they both bought, and then she ate the mouse.*

Now ask the student the general question, "Can you give me a brief summary of this passage?" The student should answer by summarizing the plot, rather than listing details. Her answer should be no more than three sentences and should resemble one of the following:

> "A cat and a mouse set up house together. They bought a pot of fat for the winter, but the cat pretended to go to christenings and ate the entire thing. When the mouse found out, the cat ate her."
>
> "A cat and a mouse bought a pot of fat and hid it in a church. The cat told the mouse that she had to go to three christenings. Each time she went out, she ate some of the fat, until it was all gone."
>
> "The cat told the mouse that she was going to the christenings of three babies. She said that they were named Top-off, Half-done, and All-gone. But she had really eaten the pot of fat—first the top, then half, then the rest of it."

If she has difficulty condensing the story, ask the following three questions:

> What did the cat and the mouse do together?
>
> In one sentence, how did the cat trick the mouse?
>
> What happened at the end of the story?

Then have the student repeat her answers in order; this will form her brief summary. Write down the student's narration on the lines below, but do not allow her to watch.

____

____

____

____

Then choose one or two sentences (about 12–15 words) to dictate back to the student. Repeat the sentences twice and ask the student to repeat them back to you before she writes on Student Workbook page 7. If she cannot repeat the sentences, read them again until she is able to keep them in mind.

Give all necessary help in spelling and punctuation.

When done, set the workbook page aside for the next lesson, which is on the back of it.

Day Four: Dictation Exercise *Student Workbook page 8*

***Focus:** Comma and period use*

Pull out Student Workbook page 8. Ask the student to write her name and the date.

Tell the student that today's dictation sentences are from the Grimms' fairy tale called "Hansel and Gretel." In "Hansel and Gretel," two children lost in the wood stumble into a clearing—and see a house all made out of candy and cake. They are so hungry that they decide to taste it!

Dictate the following sentences to the student two times. Before you read, tell the student that you will indicate commas by pausing, and the period by pausing for a longer time. When you read, be sure to let your voice drop to indicate the end of each sentence.

> Hansel broke off a piece of the roof, which was made of cake. Gretel nibbled on a pane of sugar glass.

Ask the student to repeat the sentences back to you before she writes. Remind her to pause at the commas and periods. If she cannot remember the entire selection, you may repeat it additional times.

Watch the student as she writes, and correct her at once if she begins to make a mistake. You may need to help her spell the proper names.

Day Five (optional): Creative Writing *Student Workbook page 9*

As discussed in the introduction, the fifth lesson of each week is an optional creative writing lesson/ prompt. Please refer to page vii for detailed instructions on how to use these prompts.

For creative writing activities in weeks 1-10, student responses to the prompt should be one sentence of roughly 12-15 words. If your student's verbal response is longer than 15 words, shorten it before writing it down.

Pull out Student Workbook page 9. Write the student's name and the date for him as he watches, or ask him to write the name and date independently. Before providing the prompt, reread the pourquoi tale on Student Workbook pages 1–2.

> **Instructor:** Imagine that you meet the Straw, the Coal, and the Bean while they are on their journey. How would you help them get across the river without getting hurt? (You can answer this question for all three characters, or for just one if you prefer!) Remember to capitalize proper names when writing down your answer. If you like, draw a picture of the Straw, the Coal, and the Bean to illustrate your story.

WEEK 2

DAY ONE: Narration Exercise *Student pages 11–13*

Focus: *Identifying the central theme in a selection*

Pull out Student pages 11–12 and 13. Ask the student to write his name and the date on Student page 13.

Allow the student to read the story on Student pages 11–12, either silently or aloud. Before he begins, pronounce the name Scheherazade for him (Shu-hair-ah-zahd).

After the student reads, you may want to explain that the names of three of the ships in the story are jokes. Use the following information:

Implacable is a good name for a ship; an "implacable" enemy is an enemy who cannot be soothed or made less hostile. "Placable" comes from the Latin word *placare*, which means "to appease"—to make peace with. You can make peace with a placable enemy, but not with an implacable enemy; adding "im" to "placable" makes the word mean the opposite.

Incapable is a joke. Someone who is "capable" is *able* to do things. If you tell a capable person to clean up the dishes after dinner, the dishes will be washed, dried, and put neatly away. But adding "in," just like adding "im," makes the word mean the opposite. Naming a ship *Incapable* is like naming it "Useless."

If something is "possible," it can be done. Something "impossible" is the opposite—it can't be done.

Plausible means "believable, reasonable, apparently true." An "implausible" story is fanciful and unlikely.

Now help the student begin to identify the central theme in the selection by asking the following questions. He should try to answer these questions without looking back at the story, but if he cannot remember an answer after thinking for a few minutes, allow him to reread. Remind him to answer in complete sentences.

Instructor: Did Scheherazade have a good journey in the hold of the *Glorious*?
Student: *No, it was a very bad journey.*

Instructor: Tell me three things that were terrible about the ship's hold.
Student: *There was no light or air; the hay was moldy and the grain was filled with bugs; the water was bad; rats ate the food and nibbled the horses' hooves; the stalls were never cleaned; the horses were never brushed.*

Instructor: Where did the horses' grooms come from?
Student: *They came from jails and prisons.*

Instructor: Why did the troops (the soldiers) have to be watched carefully when they were allowed to go on deck?
Student: *They tended to jump overboard.*

Instructor: Scheherazade says that by the time the ship anchored, she didn't even care that the journey was over. Why?
Student: *She was too sick and weary.*

Now say to the student, "Try to tell me, in one sentence, what Scheherazade thought of her journey to Boston." The student should respond, "The journey to Boston was horrible," OR "It was a very bad journey," OR "The journey made Scheherazade sick." Prompt the student, if he seems uncertain, by asking the first comprehension question again.

Once the student has come up with this sentence, say, "Now give me two more sentences with specific details in them about *how* the journey was horrible." The purpose of this exercise is to guide the student into stating the central theme of the passage and supporting that theme with specifics.

The answer should resemble one of the following:

> "Scheherazade had a horrible journey to Boston. The ship was dark and filled with rats. Her grain and hay were spoiled."
>
> "The journey in the ships was very bad. The horses were never cleaned or brushed, and they weren't properly fed. All of the grooms came from jails and prisons."
>
> "The journey made Scheherazade sick. She didn't have enough food, light, or air. The journey was so awful that some of the soldiers jumped overboard."

Write down the student's narration on Student page 13 as he watches.

When done, set the workbook page aside for the next lesson, which is on the back of it.

Day Two: Dictation Exercise *Student page 14*

Focus: *Formation of plural nouns*

Pull out Student page 14. Ask the student to write his name and the date.

Tell the student that today's dictation sentence is from the book *Mr. Revere and I.* When Scheherazade first comes from England, she believes that the American rebels are simple farmers who aren't very intelligent, and who certainly know nothing about proper fighting.

Before you read the sentence, tell the student that the sentence has a *semicolon* in it. Remind him that a semicolon is used to separate two complete sentences. It acts like a period, but unlike a period, a semicolon tells you that the second sentence will be so closely related to the first sentence that they belong together. The first word that comes after the semicolon isn't capitalized (unlike the first word that comes after a period). Tell the student to listen for the end of the first complete sentence, where you will pause to indicate the semicolon.

As you read, be sure to let your voice fall slightly to indicate the ending of the complete sentence that comes before the semicolon.

Read the sentence twice as the student listens.

> Of course they could shoot; any bumpkins who lived mostly on squirrels, rabbits, deer and wild turkeys would have to be able to shoot.

Ask the student to repeat the sentence back to you.

Then tell the student that you will read the sentence a third time. This time, the student should listen for the commas that separate items in a list. He should raise his hand or tap the table every time you reach a comma.

On this third reading, pause significantly at each comma, but make sure that your pause at the semicolon is *longer*. If the student indicates that he hears a comma after the word "deer," explain that items in a list can be separated *either* by conjunctions (*but, and, or*) or by commas. It is not necessary to use both.

Watch the student as he writes, and correct him at once if he begins to make a mistake.

When he is finished, ask him to point out each plural noun. As he points, tell him the rule that governs each plural.

bumpkins	Most nouns form the plural by adding an *s*
rabbits	Most nouns form the plural by adding an *s*
squirrels	Most nouns form the plural by adding an *s*
deer	Irregular noun; the singular and plural are the same
turkeys	Form the plural of a noun ending in *y* by adding an *s* if the *y* is preceded by a vowel.

Day Three: Narration and Dictation *Student pages 15–17*

Focus: *Identifying the central emotion in a passage and writing original sentences from dictation*

Pull out Student pages 15–16 and 17. Ask the student to write his name and the date on Student page 17.

Today's exercise will combine narration and dictation. Allow the student to read the story on Student pages 15–16, either silently or aloud.

Help the student recall important details by asking the following questions. He should try to answer these questions without looking back at the story, but if he cannot remember an answer after thinking for a few minutes, allow him to reread. Remind him to answer in complete sentences.

Instructor: What did Scheherazade's cart have in it?
Student: *It was loaded with hoofs and horns.*

Instructor: The passage describes Scheherazade's food with two words; can you remember them?
Student: *Her food was atrocious and scanty. [If necessary, explain that "atrocious" means "of horrible quality" and "scanty" means "not very much."]*

Instructor: What happened to her coat?
Student: *It grew long and matted.*

Instructor: What did the collar do to her skin?
Student: *It rubbed sores.*

Instructor: What was Scheherazade's greatest fear?
Student: *She was afraid that she might see horses from her old regiment.*

Instructor: When she saw the regiment coming, what did she do?
Student: *She ran away.*

Instructor: What two things does Scheherazade say made her feel humiliated?
Student: *Pulling a glue cart and looking shabby and dirty both made her feel humiliated.*

Instructor: Her embarrassment and humiliation were so deep that she decided to do something terrible, if she ever met Ajax and her friends again. What did she mean to do?
Student: *She meant to drown herself in the harbor.*

Now say to the student, "Finish the following thought: 'Scheherazade hoped that she wouldn't see her friends because . . .'" He may use two or three sentences to complete the thought. His answer should resemble one of the following:

> "Scheherazade hoped she wouldn't see her friends because she was embarrassed. She was forced to pull a cart full of bones for making glue. Her coat was long and matted and she had collar sores."
>
> "Scheherazade hoped she wouldn't see her friends because they were still in the regiment and she was not. She was humiliated because no horse of spirit would ever pull a glue cart. She was dirty and shaggy and she had sores."

Encourage the student to use the word "embarrassed" (or "embarrassing") or the word "humiliated" in his answer.

Write down the student's narration on the lines below, but do not allow him to watch.

____

____

____

____

Then choose one or two sentences (about 12–15 words) to dictate back to the student. Repeat the sentences twice and ask the student to repeat them back to you before he writes on Student page 17. If he cannot repeat the sentences, read them again until he is able to keep them in mind.

Give all necessary help in spelling and punctuation.

When done, set the workbook page aside for the next lesson, which is on the back of it.

Day Four: Dictation Exercise *Student page 18*

***Focus:** Plural nouns, exclamations*

Pull out Student page 18. Ask the student to write his name and the date.

Tell the student that today's dictation sentences are from *Mr. Revere and I.* This is what Scheherazade says, after all of her adventures.

Dictate the following sentences to the student two times. Before you read, tell the student that there is an exclamation point at the end of one of the sentences. Be sure to indicate this with your voice. Pause at the comma in the second sentence.

> How times and fortunes do change! My circumstances are most comfortable, my duties almost none.

Ask the student to repeat the sentences back to you before he writes. Remind him to put the exclamation point in the proper place. If he cannot remember the entire selection, you may repeat it additional times.

Watch the student as he writes, and correct him at once if he begins to make a mistake. Give all necessary spelling help.

When the student is finished writing, tell him that there are four plural nouns in these sentences. Three of them formed the plural by adding an *s*, but the fourth followed another rule. Ask him to find all four nouns and to tell you which three simply added an *s* (times, fortunes, circumstances).

Ask the student to write the singular form of the fourth noun (duty) underneath the plural form (duties). Remind the student that when a noun ends in *y* preceded by a consonant, you form the plural by changing the *y* to *i* and adding *-es.*

Day Five (optional): Creative Writing *Student page 19*

Pull out Student page 19. Write the student's name and the date for her as she watches, or ask her to write the name and date independently.

> **Instructor:** Scheherazade traveled across the Atlantic Ocean on a ship with many other horses. What animal would you choose to have if you had to have ten of them? Make sure to use the correct plural form when writing your answer. You can write just one sentence explaining which animals you chose, or add another sentence explaining why you love them or how you play with them! If you like, draw a picture of yourself surrounded by your pets!

WEEK 3

Day One: Narration Exercise *Student pages 21–23*

***Focus:** Identifying the central details in a description*

Pull out Student pages 21–22 and Student page 23. Ask the student to write her name and the date on Student page 23.

Allow the student to read the story on Student pages 21–22, either silently or aloud.

Help the student begin to identify the central details in the narrative by asking the following questions. She should try to answer these questions without looking back at the story, but if she cannot remember an answer after thinking for a few minutes, allow her to reread. Remind her to answer in complete sentences.

Instructor: Do you remember one of the two things mentioned in the passage that ships unloaded?
Student: *The ships unloaded turtles and chandeliers.*

Instructor: Do you remember two of the three things that street vendors sold?
Student: *They sold fever pills, hair oil, and oysters.*

Instructor: List three other things that Paul Revere could see in Boston.
Student: *He could see traveling acrobats, performing monkeys, parades, firework displays, fistfights, a pickled pirate's head, and a polar bear.*

Instructor: List five things that Paul Revere made out of silver.
Student: *He made beads, rings, lockets, bracelets, buttons, medals, pitchers, teapots, spoons, sugar basins, cups, ewers, porringers, shoe buckles, candlesticks, and a squirrel collar.*

Instructor: What did Paul Revere do at Christ Church to make extra money?
Student: *He rang the bells.*

Instructor: List four different times or reasons when the bells were rung.
Student: *They were rung on Sundays, three times a day on weekdays [that only counts as one answer!], holidays, anniversaries, fires, emergencies, deaths, good news, bad news.*

Instructor: Paul did six more things to earn extra money. Can you remember at least three?
Student: *He engraved portraits, sold pictures, made picture frames, brought out hymnbooks, and became a dentist.*

Instructor: What did he make false teeth out of?
Student: *He whittled them out of hippopotamus tusk.*

Now ask the student the general question, "Can you give me a brief summary of this passage?" The student should answer by listing details about Paul Revere's busy life. Her answer should be no more than three sentences and should resemble one of the following:

> "Paul Revere was a silversmith who made rings, bracelets, teapots, spoons, and cups. He rang the bells at Christ Church to make extra money. He also sold pictures, made picture frames, and became a dentist."
>
> "Paul Revere lived in a very busy place—Boston. In Boston, you could always see something exciting going on, like fireworks, a parade, or performing monkeys. Paul Revere was a silversmith, but he also rang church bells, made artificial teeth, and sold pictures."
>
> "Paul Revere was a silversmith, but that's not all he did. He also rang the Christ Church bells every time there was a special occasion. He made false teeth out of hippopotamus tusks, sold hymnbooks, engraved portraits, and made picture frames."

Write down the student's narration on Student page 23 as she watches.

When done, set the workbook page aside for the next lesson, which is on the back of it.

Day Two: Dictation Exercise *Student page 24*

Focus: *Plural nouns*

Pull out Student page 24. Ask the student to write her name and the date.

Tell the student that today's dictation sentences are from another biography of Paul Revere, *Paul Revere, American Patriot* by JoAnne Grote.

Dictate the following sentences to the student two times. Before you read, tell the student that there are two commas and two periods. Pause briefly at the commas and for a long time at the first period.

> Many huge wooden docks, called wharves, lined the harbor. Paul's family lived on a wharf when he was seven.

Now ask the student to repeat the sentences back to you before she writes. If she cannot remember the entire selection, you may repeat it additional times.

Watch the student as she writes, and correct her at once if she begins to make a mistake. You may need to help her with the spellings "wharf" and "wharves"; also remind her, if necessary, that "Paul's" is a possessive noun, and that it ends with an apostrophe and an *s*.

When she is finished, point out that "wharves" is the plural form of "wharf." To make a plural out of a noun ending in *f*, you often change the *f* to a *v* and add *-es*.

Day Three: Narration and Dictation *Student pages 25–26*

***Focus:** Identifying the central narrative thread in a passage and writing original sentences from dictation*

Pull out Student pages 25 and 26. Ask the student to write her name and the date on Student page 26.

Today's exercise will combine narration and dictation. Allow the student to read the story on Student page 25, either silently or aloud.

Help the student begin to identify the central thread in the narrative by asking the following questions. She should try to answer these questions without looking back at the story, but if she cannot remember an answer after thinking for a few minutes, allow her to reread. Remind her to answer in complete sentences.

Instructor: What kind of cargo were the British ships carrying, as they sailed towards American ports?
Student: *They were carrying tea.*

Instructor: When the *Dartmouth* arrived in Boston, how did the Sons of Liberty keep the owner from unloading the tea?
Student: *They stood guard with muskets and bayonets.*

Instructor: What message did Paul Revere carry to a nearby seaport?
Student: *The message was that British tea ships might try to unload.*

Instructor: How did the Sons of Liberty disguise themselves?
Student: *They dressed like Indians and put soot and lamp black on their faces.*

Instructor: What did they do with the tea?
Student: *They threw the tea into the harbor.*

Now ask the student the general question, "Can you give me a brief summary of this passage?" The student should answer by summarizing the plot, rather than listing details. Her answer should be no more than three sentences and should resemble one of the following:

> "British ships filled with tea docked in Boston. The Sons of Liberty refused to let the owners unload the tea. That night, they dressed up like Indians, went on board the ships, and threw the tea into the water."
>
> "The Sons of Liberty refused to let tea ships unload, and sent messages to other seaports so that no ships could unload anywhere else. After dark, they dressed up like Indians and blackened their faces. Then they boarded the ships, broke open the tea chests, and threw the tea into the water."
>
> "The Sons of Liberty decided to keep British tea ships from unloading. Paul Revere helped carry the message to other seaports. Once it was dark, the Sons of Liberty disguised themselves, went aboard the ships, and threw all of the tea into the harbor."

Write down the student's narration on the lines below, but do not allow her to watch.

Then choose one or two sentences (about 12–15 words) to dictate back to the student. Repeat the sentences twice and ask the student to repeat them back to you before she writes on Student page 26. If she cannot repeat the sentences, read them again until she is able to keep them in mind.

Give all necessary help in spelling and punctuation.

Day Four: Dictation Exercise

Student page 27

Focus: *Exclamations, plural nouns*

Pull out Student page 27. Ask the student to write her name and the date.

Tell the student that today's dictation sentences are from a song written to celebrate the Boston Tea Party, when Paul Revere and many others threw tea from England into the Boston Harbor rather than pay taxes on it.

Ask the student if she can decide what punctuation marks come at the end of these sentences. When you read the sentences, use an excited voice.

> Bring out your axes! And tell King George we'll pay no taxes on his foreign tea!

Ask the student to repeat the sentences back to you before she writes. If she cannot remember the entire selection, you may repeat it additional times.

Watch the student as she writes, and correct her at once if she begins to make a mistake. You may need to remind her that "King George" is a proper name, and that both words should be capitalized. You may also need to remind the student that "we'll" is a contraction of "we will," and that the apostrophe shows that the letters *wi* have been left out. If the student needs help spelling "foreign," remind her of the rule: I before E, except after C, or when sounded like A, as in "neighbor" and "weigh." Americans tend to swallow the last syllable of the word "foreign" (so that it sounds like "forn"), but if the student says the second syllable on its own ("reign"), she will hear the A sound.

When the student is finished, ask her to write the singular nouns "ax" and "tax" above or below the plural nouns "axes" and "taxes." Remind that student that nouns ending in *x*, *sh*, and *ch* form the plural by adding *-es* rather than just *-s*.

When done, set the workbook page aside for the next lesson, which is on the back of it.

Day Five (optional): Creative Writing *Student page 28*

Pull out Student page 28. Write the student's name and the date for him as he watches, or ask him to write the name and date independently.

> **Instructor:** Paul Revere had many jobs to help him make enough money for his family. Imagine you are old enough to have a job. What is one thing you would like to try doing to make money? Or what is one thing you would make and sell? If you like, draw a picture of the thing you would make or the job you would have.

WEEK 4

Day One: Narration Exercise *Student pages 29–31*

***Focus:** Identifying the central narrative thread in a passage*

Pull out Student pages 29–30 and 31. Ask the student to write his name and the date on Student page 31.

Allow the student to read the story on Student pages 29–30, either silently or aloud.

Help the student begin to identify the central thread in the narrative by asking the following questions. He should try to answer these questions without looking back at the story, but if he cannot remember an answer after thinking for a few minutes, allow him to reread. Remind him to answer in complete sentences.

Instructor: What did Homer, Freddy, and Louis see standing in front of the theater?
***Student:** They saw the Super-Duper's car.*

Instructor: Tell me two things you remember about the car.
***Student:** It was long and red, it had chromium trimmings, it had the Super-Duper's monogram on the side. [You may need to explain that a monogram is a fancy way of writing a person's initials.]*

Instructor: What did Freddy ask the Super-Duper to do?
***Student:** He asked the Super-Duper to fly or bend horse shoes.*

Instructor: Did the Super-Duper do either of those things?
***Student:** No, he did not.*

Instructor: In the movie about the Super-Duper, what happened when the villain turned the electric ray on the Super-Duper?
***Student:** Nothing happened.*

Instructor: How did the Super-Duper get rid of the electric ray machine?
***Student:** He threw it over a cliff.*

Instructor: What did the Super-Duper do when he drove up behind old Lucy and the wagon?
***Student:** He honked his horn and then he passed the wagon.*

Instructor: What did Homer say about the Super-Duper's driving?
***Student:** He said that the Super-Duper was driving too fast.*

Instructor: What did the boys hear at the end of the story?
***Student:** They heard a loud crash.*

Now ask the student the general question, "Can you give me a brief summary of this passage?" The student should answer by summarizing the plot, rather than listing details. His answer should be no more than four sentences and should resemble one of the following:

> "Freddy, Homer, and Louis went to see a movie about the Super-Duper. The Super-Duper's car was standing outside the movie theater. After they saw the movie, the boys were driving home when the Super-Duper's car passed them. The car was going too fast, and soon the boys heard a loud crash."
>
> "Homer and his friends were fans of the Super-Duper. They got to meet him and see his car. After they left the movie theater, the Super-Duper's car passed them on the way home. Homer said that the Super-Duper was driving too fast. Right away, they heard a crash."
>
> "Homer and Freddy and Freddy's little brother met the Super-Duper when they went to see a movie about him. In the movie, the Super-Duper threw an electric ray machine over a cliff. On the way home, the Super-Duper drove past the boys, going too fast. Next, the boys heard a loud crash."

The student will probably attempt to put too much information into the summary. If he has difficulty condensing the story, ask the following three questions:

> Who are the three main characters, and what did they do together for fun?
>
> What did they see?
>
> What happened when they left the movie theater?

Then have the student repeat his answers in order; this will form his brief summary.

Write down the student's narration on Student page 31 as he watches.

When done, set the workbook page aside for the next lesson, which is on the back of it.

Day Two: Dictation Exercise — *Student page 32*

***Focus:** Pronouns, exclamations*

Pull out Student page 32. Ask the student to write his name and the date.

Tell the student that today's dictation sentence is from a book called *The Science of Superheroes* by Lois Gresh and Robert Weinberg. The authors try to find scientific explanations for the powers of imaginary superheroes like Superman and the Super-Duper.

First, the writers tell us that, in the old comic books, "Superman's tremendous strength was the result of being born on a high gravity planet. Earth's gravity was much weaker than that of Krypton, so Superman was able to lift heavy objects due to the difference in gravitational fields." Then they quote from one of those comic books. That quote is today's dictation sentence.

Dictate the following sentence to the student two times. Before you read, tell the student to listen carefully to your tone of voice to decide what the ending punctuation should be. Be sure to use an excited tone of voice to indicate the exclamation point, and pause significantly at the commas. Do not tell the student that you are pausing at the commas; he should now begin to hear these pauses on his own.

> If you were on a world smaller than ours, you could jump over high buildings, lift enormous weights, and thus duplicate some of the feats of the Man of Steel!

Now ask the student to repeat the sentence back to you before he writes. If he cannot remember the entire sentence, you may repeat it additional times.

Watch the student as he writes, and correct him at once if he begins to make a mistake. If he does not put in the commas, stop him and read the sentence again with exaggerated pauses. Ask him what punctuation mark he should use to indicate the pauses.

When he is finished, tell him to point to the words "you" and "ours." Tell him that these are *pronouns*: words that take the place of nouns.

You may also tell the student the book's conclusion: for Superman to be as strong as he is, Krypton would have to be three times as dense as the sun. So far as we know, this isn't possible!

Day Three: Narration and Dictation — *Student pages 33–35*

***Focus:** Identifying the central theme in a selection and writing original sentences from dictation*

Today's exercise will combine narration and dictation. Allow the student to read the story on Student pages 33–34, either silently or aloud.

Help the student begin to identify the central theme in the selection by asking the following questions. He should try to answer these questions without looking back at the story, but if he cannot remember an answer after thinking for a few minutes, allow him to reread. Remind him to answer in complete sentences.

Instructor: Where was the Super-Duper's car?
Student: *The car was in a ditch.*

Instructor: How did the boys expect the Super-Duper to get the car out?
Student: *They expected him to lift it out with one hand.*

Instructor: What was the Super-Duper doing?
Student: *He was sitting with his head in his hands.*

Instructor: The story mentions several of the Super-Duper's superpowers. What did he do to battleships?
Student: *He broke them up like toothpicks.*

Instructor: What did cannon-balls do to the Super-Duper?
Student: *They bounced off his chest.*

Instructor: What did the Super-Duper say?
Student: *He said "Ouch."*

Instructor: Why did he say "Ouch"?
Student: *He got caught on a barbed-wire fence.*

Instructor: How did they get the car out of the ditch?
Student: *Lucy pulled it back onto the road.*

Now ask the student the general question, "Can you give me a brief summary of this passage?" The student should answer by summarizing the theme, rather than listing details. His answer should be no more than three sentences and should resemble one of the following:

> "The boys thought that the Super-Duper would be able to lift his car out of the ditch with one hand. Instead, he got caught in barbed wire and needed help. They realized that the Super-Duper wasn't really a super-hero."
>
> "Homer and Freddy and Louis saw the Super-Duper's car in a ditch. They thought he would lift it out with one hand. Instead, the Super-Duper got caught in barbed wire and asked the boys to help him find a garage."
>
> "The boys thought that the Super-Duper was so tough that cannon-balls bounced off his chest. But when the Super-Duper's car ran into a ditch, he couldn't even get it out by himself. The old horse had to pull it out instead."

If he has difficulty condensing the story, ask the following three questions:

> What did the boys think about the Super-Duper before his car crashed?
>
> What happened to the Super-Duper?
>
> What did the boys think about the Super-Duper after that?

Then have the student repeat his answers in order; this will form his brief summary. Write down the student's narration on the lines below, but do not allow him to watch.

____

____

____

____

Then choose one or two sentences (about 12–15 words) to dictate back to the student. Repeat the sentences twice and ask the student to repeat them back to you before he writes on Student page 35. If he cannot repeat the sentences, read them again until he is able to keep them in mind.

Give all necessary help in spelling and punctuation.

When done, set the workbook page aside for the next lesson, which is on the back of it.

Day Four: Dictation Exercise *Student page 36*

***Focus:** Pronouns*

Pull out Student page 36. Ask the student to write his name and the date.

Tell the student that today's dictation sentences are from a book called *Krypton* by Janey Levy. Also tell the student that although Superman is supposed to be tougher than the Super-Duper, one thing can bring him down. Read the student this paragraph from the book *Krypton*: "The word 'krypton' may make you think of Superman. Krypton was the name of his home planet, and kryptonite was the mineral that could drain his superpowers. Given its association with a fictional superhero, it may surprise you to learn there really is a krypton (Kr). It is not a planet, though. It is a chemical element, a gas that belongs to a group of gases called the noble or inert gases."

Now dictate the following sentences to the student two times. Before you read, tell the student that there are three separate sentences in the selection, each ending with a period.

> Krypton looks just like air. It is colorless, odorless, and tasteless. It is also harmless.

Ask the student to repeat the sentences back to you before he writes. If he cannot remember the entire selection, you may repeat it additional times.

Watch the student as he writes, and correct him at once if he begins to make a mistake. You may need to help him with the spelling of "krypton."

When the student is finished writing, ask him to circle the first "it." This is a pronoun. Ask the student to draw an arrow back to the word "it" stands for (krypton). Ask him to do the same with the second "it" (the second arrow should also point back to "krypton").

Day Five (optional): Creative Writing *Student page 37*

Pull out Student page 37. Write the student's name and the date for her as she watches, or ask her to write the name and date independently.

Instructor: In the story, Homer Price and his friend Freddy help out the Super-Duper. Think of a time when you did something kind for someone. Tell me about it. Or tell me about a time when a friend did something kind for you. If you like, draw an illustration to go with the story.

WEEK 5

Day One: Poetry Exercise *Student pages 39–40*

***Focus:** Definitions of poetic terms*

Pull out Student pages 39 and 40. Ask the student to write her name and the date on page 39.

Allow the student to read the poem on Student pages 39–40, either silently or aloud.

Tell the student that, instead of asking questions about the poem, you are going to discuss it with her.

Note: It is not necessary for the student to memorize (or even fully understand) everything that follows. This is simply an introduction to poetry; the concepts will be presented again and again so that the student has a chance to master them.

Look at the poem with the student and point out the following. Definitions are provided on Student page 40.

1. This poem is written in "quatrains." A quatrain is a set of four lines that belong together.
2. You can discover the "rhyme scheme" (the pattern of rhyming words) within each quatrain by finding the words that rhyme with each other and giving each rhyming sound a different letter of the alphabet as its name. Look at the first quatrain of the poem. The word "toves" is at the end of the first line, so we give the ending sound "oves" the letter A as its name. The word "wabe" is at the end of the second line, so we give the ending sound "abe" the letter B as its name. The word "borogoves" is at the end of the third line. It ends with the sound "oves," so we give that sound its name: A. The word "outgrabe" is at the end of the fourth line. It ends with the sound "abe," so we give that sound its name: B.

The rhyme scheme for the first quatrain is ABAB.

Now ask the student to fill in the rhyme pattern for the second quatrain. She should come up with ABAB for this quatrain as well; "son" and "shun" are A rhymes, "catch" and "snatch" are B rhymes.

Look at the third quatrain. We give the rhyming sound "and" (as in hand) the name A. "Ought" (as in "sought") is B. "Tree" ends with a new sound, "ee." Since this doesn't rhyme with either A or B, we have to call it C. The fourth line ends with the "ought" sound again, so the rhyme pattern is ABCB.

Now ask the student to fill in the rhyme pattern for the next four quatrains. The correct answers are:

Fourth quatrain	ABAB
Fifth quatrain	ABCB (If the student points out that "dead" and "head" rhyme, you may tell her that this is called an "internal rhyme.")
Sixth quatrain	ABCB
Seventh quatrain	ABAB

3. Tell the student that you are now going to talk about "meter." Before she can understand meter, though, she will have to understand three new words.

The first word is "syllable." This may not be a new word for the student, but if she is unfamiliar with it, explain that a "syllable" is a part of a word containing one vowel sound. Read the following words to the student and ask the student to clap once for each vowel sound:

baseball	base	ball		two syllables
airplane	air	plane		two syllables
drumbeat	drum	beat		two syllables
elephant	el	e	phant	three syllables

The second word is "stress." When you "stress" part of a word, you let your voice emphasize that part of it. Read the words again, this time emphasizing the bolded syllable:

baseball

airplane

drumbeat

elephant

Explain that in each of these words, the stress falls on the first syllable. Read the words again, stressing the last syllable instead, and ask the student whether the words sound right. (The answer should be "no.")

The third word is "foot." In poetry, a "foot" is a certain number of syllables that always fall into the same pattern of stresses. These patterns create rhythms that help make a poem a poem.

Ask the student to read the lines from the poem printed on Student page 40 aloud, stressing the bolded syllables with her voice. After she reads, point out that the syllables always fall into the same pattern:

unstress **stress**

unstress **stress**

unstress **stress**

In this poem, each "foot" has two syllables, and those syllables always fall into the pattern "unstress **stress**."

Ask the student to circle each foot in the quatrain on Student page 40. Her quatrain should look like this:

One, **two!** One, **two!** And **through** and **through**
The **vor**pal **blade** went **snick**er-**snack!**
He **left** it **dead**, and **with** its **head**
He **went** ga**lumph**ing **back**.

Tell her that this pattern (sets of two syllables in the pattern "unstress **stress**") is called **iambic.** Anytime a poem uses this particular rhythm, we say that the meter is iambic. "Meter" is the word we use to refer to the rhythm of a poem.

Optional: for students who are comfortable with identifying parts of speech.

Even though so many words in the poem are made up, you can still tell what part of speech each word is. "Slithy" and "toves" are both made-up words, but if you know that "slithy toves" are "gyring and gimbling," you know that "toves" has to be a noun. The toves are **doing** the verbs in the sentence, so they have to be persons, things, or animals. "Slithy" describes "toves." We know that a word that describes a noun is an adjective, so "slithy" must be an adjective.

DAY TWO: Dictation Exercise *Student page 41*

Focus: *Action verbs*

Pull out Student page 41. Ask the student to write her name and the date.

Tell the student that today's dictation sentence is also from *Through the Looking-Glass* by Lewis Carroll. In these two sentences, Humpty Dumpty is explaining to Alice what some of the words in "Jabberwocky" mean.

Dictate the following sentences to the student two times. Before you read, tell the student that you will pause significantly at each comma, but that you will pause even longer at the period that separates the two sentences. Also tell the student to listen for the word "they're." Explain that this is the contraction for "they are," not the adverb "there." If necessary, remind the student to put an apostrophe where letters are left out of the contraction.

> Toves are something like badgers, they're something like lizards, and they're something like corkscrews. They make their nests under sundials and live on cheese.

Now ask the student to repeat the sentences back to you before she writes. If she cannot repeat both sentences, you may repeat them additional times.

Watch the student as she writes, and correct her at once if she begins to make a mistake. When she is finished, point out that there are two different kinds of verbs in these sentences. The verb "are" is a *linking verb*. It links "toves" to "something." The verbs "make" and "live" are *action verbs*.

DAY THREE: Poetry Exercise *Student page 43*

Focus: *Definitions of poetic terms*

Pull out Student page 43. Ask the student to write his name and the date.

Allow the student to read the poem on Student page 43, either silently or aloud.

Tell the student that, instead of asking questions about the poem, you are going to discuss it with her.

This poem is written in sets of four lines. Ask the student if she can remember the name for a set of four lines that belong together. If necessary, remind her that the name is "quatrain." Help her to write "quatrain" on Line 1 below the poem.

Ask the student to give each ending rhyme a letter, as she did for "Jabberwocky." She should write these letters in the blanks at the end of the lines. The pattern is:

A
B
A
B

A
B
A
B

Remind her that this is called a "rhyme scheme."

Now ask the student to read the two lines written below Line 1 out loud, stressing each bolded syllable.

When she is finished, tell her that this is the opposite of iambic meter. Iambic meter falls into this pattern: unstress **stress**. Help the student to write "iambic" on Line 2, after the words "unstress **stress**."

In this poem, each pair of syllables falls into the pattern **stress** unstress. Ask the student to circle each "foot" in the two lines she just read. Remind her that in this poem, each foot is two syllables. Her answer should look like this:

(**Ste**go)(**sau**rus)(**blund**ered)(**calm**ly)(**through** the)(**pre**his)(**tor**ic) **scene**,
(**ne**ver)(**caus**ing)(**an**y)(**o**ther)(**crea**ture) **woe.**

This is called "trochaic" meter: a stressed syllable followed by an unstressed syllable. You will probably need to point out to the student that Jack Prelutsky ends each line with a half foot: he drops the second, unstressed syllable in each final foot because it makes the poem sound choppier, like a stegosaurus lumbering and blundering along.

When done, set the workbook page aside for the next lesson, which is on the back of it.

Day Four: Dictation Exercise *Student page 44*

***Focus:** Poetic form*

Pull out Student page 44. Ask the student to write her name and the date.

Tell the student that today's dictation exercise is from the poem "The Walrus and the Carpenter," found in Lewis Carroll's book *Through the Looking-Glass*. Begin by reading the first stanza of the poem to the student:

> The sun was shining on the sea,
> Shining with all his might,
> He did his very best to make
> The billows smooth and bright—
> And this was odd, because it was
> The middle of the night.
> The moon was shining sulkily,
> Because she thought the sun
> Had got no business to be there
> After the day was done—
> "It's very rude of him," she said,
> "To come and spoil the fun!"

Now read the first four lines to the student, emphasizing the bolded syllables:

> The **sun** was **shin**ing **on** the **sea**,
>
> Shi**ning** with **all** his **might**,
>
> He **did** his **very** **best** to **make**
>
> The **bil**lows **smooth** and **bright—**

Remind her that this is iambic meter; each pair of syllables falls into the pattern "unstress **stress.**"

Now remind the student that, in poetry, each line begins directly underneath the previous line, and each line begins with a capital letter. Read these four lines twice more, pausing significantly at the end of each line. Now ask the student to repeat them back to you, reproducing your pauses. If she cannot remember all four lines, repeat them additional times.

Tell the student to stop at the end of each line so that you can tell her the proper punctuation (do not expect her to guess, correctly, that the first two lines end with commas and the last ends with a dash—there's no way she could know this). Watch her as she writes, and correct her at once if she begins to make a mistake.

Day Five (optional): Creative Writing *Student page 45*

Pull out Student page 45. Write the student's name and the date for him as he watches, or ask him to write the name and date independently.

> **Instructor:** The Jabberwocky poem is full of nonsense words. Make up your own poem with at least two lines. You can make up nonsense words; just make sure that the words at the end of each line rhyme.

WEEK 6

Day One: Narration Exercise *Student pages 47–49*

Focus: *Identifying the central narrative thread in a passage*

Pull out Student pages 47–48 and 49. Ask the student to write his name on Student page 49.

Allow the student to read the story on Student pages 47–48, either silently or aloud.

Help the student begin to identify the central elements in the narrative by asking the following questions. He should try to answer these questions without looking back at the story, but if he cannot remember an answer after thinking for a few minutes, allow him to reread. Remind him to answer in complete sentences.

Instructor: Where did the oarsmen take Jason and Gareth?
Student: *The oarsmen took them to the Great House.*

Instructor: Can you name two of the three things that King Neter-Khet did in the first few minutes that Jason was at the Great House?
Student: *He declared wars, signed peace treaties, and began a new pyramid.*

Instructor: When the Chief Scribe approached one of the clerks and told him to record the addition of grain, oil, and gold, what else did he add to the list of the Pharoah's possessions?
Student: *He added one black cat.*

Instructor: What did Jason say when he heard this?
Student: *He said that his cat was not one of Pharaoh's possessions.*

Instructor: Where did Jason and the cat go as soon as Jason protested?
Student: *Jason was put in a tiny room, and the Chief Scribe took the cat away.*

Instructor: Did Jason stay in the tiny room?
Student: *No, two guards came and got him.*

Instructor: Where did the two guards take him?
Student: *They took him to King Neter-Khet.*

Instructor: Who was sitting in front of the throne?
Student: *Gareth the cat was sitting in front of the throne.*

Now ask the student the general question, "Can you give me a brief summary of this passage?" The student should answer by summarizing the plot, rather than listing details. His answer should be no more than three sentences and should resemble one of the following:

> "Gareth and Jason were taken to the Great House of King Neter-Khet. The Chief Scribe took Gareth away, and Jason was shut up in a tiny room. But before long, guards came and got Jason and took him to the throne room."

"The Chief Scribe said that Gareth was one of King Neter-Khet's possessions. Jason tried to protect Gareth, but he was shoved into a tiny room. He stayed in the room for just a little while, and then guards took him to see King Neter-Khet and Gareth."

"The Chief Scribe took Gareth for the king and shut Jason in a cell. Before long, though, guards came to get Jason and took him to see King Neter-Khet. He saw Gareth there, sitting in front of the throne."

If the student has difficulty condensing the selection, ask him the following three questions:

What happened to Gareth?

How did Jason react?

When did Jason see Gareth again?

Then have the student repeat his answer in order; this will form his brief summary.
Write down the student's narration on Student page 49 as he watches.
When done, set the workbook page aside for the next lesson, which is on the back of it.

Day Two: Dictation Exercise *Student page 50*

***Focus:** Possessive adjectives*

Pull out Student page 50. Ask the student to write his name and the date.

Tell the student that today's dictation sentences are from Rudyard Kipling's story "The Cat That Walked by Himself" from the *Just So Stories*. Read the student the first paragraph of the story:

> Hear and attend and listen; for this befell and behappened and became and was, O my Best Beloved, when the tame animals were wild. The Dog was wild, and the Horse was wild, and the Cow was wild, and the Sheep was wild, and the Pig was wild—as wild as wild could be—and they walked in the Wet Wild Woods by their wild lones. But the wildest of all the wild animals was the Cat. He walked by himself and all places were alike to him.

Also tell the student that, in the story, the Dog goes to live with Man and Woman and becomes tame—but the Cat refuses to be tamed.

Dictate the following sentences to the student two times. Before you read, tell the student that this is what Woman says about the Dog after he is tamed. Tell the student that "Wild Dog" and "First Friend" are capitalized because Rudyard Kipling is using them as proper names. Also tell him that you will pause briefly at the comma and for a longer time at the first period.

> His name is not Wild Dog any more, but the First Friend, because he will be our friend for always and always and always. Take him with you when you go hunting.

Now ask the student to repeat the sentences back to you before he writes. If he cannot remember both sentences, you may repeat them additional times.

Watch the student as he writes, and correct him at once if he begins to make a mistake. When he is finished, ask him to underline the phrases "His name" and "our friend." Explain that "his" and "our" are particular kinds of adjectives. They are adjectives that answer the question *whose*. We call these *possessive adjectives*.

Day Three: Narration and Dictation — *Student pages 51–53*

Focus: *Identifying the central theme and writing original sentences from dictation*

Pull out Student pages 51–52 and 53. Ask the student to write his name and the date on Student page 53.

Today's exercise will combine narration and dictation. Allow the student to read the story on Student pages 51–52, either silently or aloud.

Now help the student begin to identify the central theme in the selection by asking the following questions. He should try to answer these questions without looking back at the story, but if he cannot remember an answer after thinking for a few minutes, allow him to reread. Remind him to answer in complete sentences.

Instructor: What did Gareth do when King Neter-Khet ordered him to play?
Student: *He did nothing OR He did not move.*

Instructor: How did Jason try to make Gareth play?
Student: *He pulled a jeweled mouse on a golden chain back and forth in front of the cat.*

Instructor: Did Gareth play with the mouse?
Student: *No, he did not.*

Instructor: What did Gareth do when King Neter-Khet ordered him to purr and be agreeable?
Student: *He did nothing OR He did not move.*

Instructor: What did Gareth do when Jason put him in the king's lap?
Student: *He leaped down OR He wriggled away and accidentally scratched the king.*

Instructor: What explanation did Jason give the king for Gareth's behavior?
Student: *He said that Gareth didn't feel like playing or being agreeable OR He said that's just the way cats are.*

Now say to the student, "Try to tell me, in one sentence, how Gareth behaved in front of the king—and why." The student should respond, "Gareth refused to play or purr because he didn't feel like it," OR "Gareth would not do what the king asked because that's just the way cats are," OR "Gareth wouldn't play or sit in the king's lap because he didn't want to." Prompt the student, if he seems uncertain, by asking the first and last comprehension questions again.

Once the student has come up with this sentence, say, "Now give me two more sentences with specific details in them about how Jason and the king tried to make Gareth obey, and for each specific detail, tell me how Gareth reacted." The purpose of this exercise is to guide the student into stating the central theme of the passage and supporting that theme with specifics.

The answer should resemble one of the following:

> "Gareth refused to play or purr because he didn't feel like it. Jason tried to get him to play with a mouse, but Gareth was in no mood for games. Jason tried to put Gareth in the king's lap, but Gareth leaped down."
>
> "Gareth would not do what the king asked because that's just the way cats are. Jason tried to put him in the king's lap, so that the king could stroke him. But Gareth jumped off and scratched the king."
>
> "Gareth wouldn't play or sit in the king's lap because he didn't want to. The Chief Scribe told Jason to make the cat play, but Jason could tell that Gareth wasn't in the mood. He put Gareth on the king's lap, but the cat wriggled away and jumped down."

Write down the student's narration on the lines below, but do not allow him to watch.

____

____

____

____

Then choose one or two sentences (about 12–15 words) to dictate back to the student. Repeat the sentences twice and ask the student to repeat them back to you before he writes on Student page 53. If he cannot repeat the sentences, read them again until he is able to keep them in mind.

Give all necessary help in spelling and punctuation.

When done, set the workbook page aside for the next lesson, which is on the back of it.

Day Four: Dictation Exercise — *Student page 54*

Focus: *Possessive adjectives*

Pull out Student page 54. Ask the student to write his name and the date.

Tell the student that today's dictation sentences are also from Rudyard Kipling's story "The Cat That Walked by Himself" from the *Just So Stories*. This is what the Cat says to Woman.

Dictate the following sentences to the student two times. Before you read, tell the student that "Cat" is capitalized because Kipling is using it as a proper name. Also tell the student that you will pause briefly at the commas and for a longer time at the first period.

> I am not a friend, and I am not a servant. I am the Cat who walks by himself, and I wish to come into your cave.

Now ask the student to repeat the sentences back to you before he writes. If he cannot remember both sentences, you may repeat them additional times.

Watch the student as he writes, and correct him at once if he begins to make a mistake. When he is finished, ask him to find and underline the possessive adjective that answers the question *whose*. (The answer is "your" in the phrase "your cave.")

Day Five (optional): Creative Writing *Student page 55*

Pull out Student page 55. Write the student's name and the date for her as she watches, or ask her to write the name and date independently.

> **Instructor:** In the story, the Pharaoh takes Jason's cat Gareth as his own. Imagine you are the pharaoh of your house for one day. You can command everyone who lives with you to do whatever you want. What would you ask them to do? If you like, draw a picture of yourself as a pharaoh.

WEEK 7

DAY ONE: Narration Exercise *Student pages 57–59*

***Focus:** Identifying the central narrative thread in a passage*

Pull out Student pages 57–58 and 59. Ask the student to write her name and the date on Student page 59.

Allow the student to read the story on Student pages 57–58, either silently or aloud.

Help the student begin to identify the central thread in the narrative by asking the following questions. She should try to answer these questions without looking back at the story, but if she cannot remember an answer after thinking for a few minutes, allow her to reread. Remind her to answer in complete sentences.

Instructor: What did Shi Huangdi mean?
Student: *It meant "First Emperor."*

Instructor: What two things did Shi Huangdi do to prevent revolt?
Student: *He sent his soldiers to guard and report on his enemies, and he burned books that might encourage his people to rebel.*

Instructor: Who lived in the north, outside the borders of China?
Student: *The ferocious tribes called Mongols lived in the north.*

Instructor: What had some of the Warring States done to keep Mongols away?
Student: *They built walls.*

Instructor: Why wouldn't the walls keep the Mongols out?
Student: *The walls had huge gaps in them.*

Instructor: What did Shi Huangdi decide to do?
Student: *He decided to build a Great Wall along China's northern border.*

Instructor: What was the problem with this plan?
Student: *There wasn't enough stone to build a Great Wall.*

Instructor: The architects found a solution to this problem. They figured out how to build a wall out of dirt in four steps. What were those four steps? [If necessary, you may allow the student to look back at the text as she answers.]
Student: *They made a wooden frame. They put the frame on the ground and filled it with dirt. Workers stamped and packed the earth until it was as hard as concrete. Then they lifted the frame up and set it on top of the packed earth.*

Now ask the student the general question, "Can you give me a brief summary of this passage?" The student should answer by telling you about the Mongols and the building of the

Great Wall. Her answer should be no more than three sentences. It should resemble one of the following:

> "Tribes were coming down from the north and attacking China. Shi Huangdi told his architects to build a Great Wall to stop them. They figured out how to make the wall out of dirt."
>
> "The First Emperor wanted to build a Great Wall to keep out the Mongols. But there wasn't enough stone. So his builders made a wooden frame, packed it with dirt, and made a dirt wall that was as hard as concrete."
>
> "The First Emperor was afraid that the Mongols would invade through gaps in the old walls. He ordered his builders to build a new wall—the Great Wall. There wasn't enough stone to make the Great Wall, so his builders made it out of packed dirt."

Write down the student's narration on Student page 59 as she watches.

When done, set the workbook page aside for the next lesson, which is on the back of it.

Day Two: Dictation Exercise *Student page 60*

***Focus:** Possessive adjectives*

Pull out Student page 60. Ask the student to write her name and the date.

Tell the student that today's dictation sentences are also from *The Story of the World, Volume 1: Ancient Times.* They describe what China was like before Shi Huangdi conquered the Warring States and united them into one country.

Dictate the following sentences to the student two times. Instead of telling the student that there are two sentences, simply pause at the period.

> China was ruled by strong warriors called warlords. Each warlord had his own, separate kingdom and his own army.

Ask the student to repeat the sentences back to you before she writes. If she cannot remember both sentences, you may repeat them additional times.

Watch the student as she writes, and correct her at once if she begins to make a mistake. When she is finished, ask her to underline the possessive adjectives that answer the question *whose.* (The answer is "his" in the phrases "his own, separate kingdom" and "his own army.")

You may also want to point out "kingdom" has three adjectives that modify it: his, own, and separate. Ask the student how may adjectives modify "army." (The answer is two: "his," and "own.")

Day Three: Narration and Dictation *Student pages 61–63*

Focus: *Identifying the central details in a passage and writing original sentences from dictation*

Pull out Student pages 61–62 and 63. Ask the student to write her name and the date on Student page 63.

Allow the student to read the story on Student pages 61–62, either silently or aloud.

Help the student begin to identify the central details in the narrative by asking the following questions. She should try to answer these questions without looking back at the story, but if she cannot remember an answer after thinking for a few minutes, allow her to reread. Remind her to answer in complete sentences.

Instructor: What did the Mongols live in?
Student: *They lived in felt tents.*

Instructor: What did they do to protect themselves from the cold?
Student: *They wore furs and leather and rubbed their skin with grease.*

Instructor: What did they eat instead of raising crops?
Student: *They ate foxes, rabbits, and other small wild creatures.*

Instructor: What did they do if they were in danger of starving?
Student: *They would open the veins of their horses and drink blood.*

Instructor: What did Genghis Khan want the separate Mongol clans to do?
Student: *He wanted them to join together and attack Beijing.*

Instructor: What was in Beijing that Genghis Khan wanted? The passage lists four things.
Student: *There were warm houses, soft beds, plenty of food, and bags of gold.*

Instructor: What did Genghis Khan tell his people about the disappearance of his rival's body?
Student: *He told them that the gods had taken the body away as punishment.*

Instructor: After that, did the Mongols follow Genghis?
Student: *Yes, they did.*

Now ask the student the general question, "Can you give me a brief summary of this passage?" The student should answer by describing the Mongols and what Genghis Khan wanted. Her answer should be no more than three sentences and should resemble one of the following:

> "The Mongols lived in felt tents and rubbed grease on their skins to protect them from the cold. They ate small wild creatures and sometimes they drank the blood of their horses. Genghis Khan wanted them to conquer the city of Beijing."
>
> "The Mongols lived in the wild, cold north. They were nomads who didn't grow crops or build houses. But Genghis Khan wanted them to conquer the rich city of Beijing."

"The Mongols lived in felt tents and wore fur and leather because it was so cold in the north. But there were warm houses and soft beds in Beijing. Genghis Khan wanted them to join together and conquer this rich city."

Write down the student's narration on the lines below, but do not allow her to watch.

____

____

____

____

Then choose one or two sentences (about 12–15 words) to dictate back to the student. Repeat the sentences twice and ask the student to repeat them back to you before she writes on Student page 63. If she cannot repeat the sentences, read them again until she is able to keep them in mind.

Give all necessary help in spelling and punctuation.

When done, set the workbook page aside for the next lesson, which is on the back of it.

Day Four: Dictation — *Student page 64*

Focus: *Possessive adjectives and hyphenated words*

Pull out Student page 64. Ask the student to write her name and the date.

Tell the student that today's dictation sentences are also from *The Story of the World, Volume 2.* After Genghis Khan's death, his grandson Kublai Khan tried to fight his way even further to the south of China, to conquer more of the Chinese empire. These sentences describe one of the problems he encountered.

Dictate the following sentences to the student two times. Before you read, tell the student that there is a hyphenated word in the first sentence. The word is "well-educated." The hyphen links together the two separate words "well" and "educated" into one single word. If necessary, write the word on the bottom of Student page 64 and show the student how to form the hyphen. Be sure to pause at the commas and to make a longer pause at the period.

> The Mongols were ferocious warriors, but the Chinese were shrewd and well-educated. Their scientists had developed new weapons to defend against invasion. They knew how to make poisonous fogs which could be blown across a battlefield.

Ask the student to repeat the sentence back to you before she writes. If she cannot remember the entire selection, you may repeat it additional times. This is a longer dictation selection, intended to stretch the student's ability, and if necessary you may break it into two parts.

Watch the student as she writes, and correct her at once if she begins to make a mistake. You may need to help her spell "ferocious" and "poisonous."

When she is finished, ask her to find and underline the possessive adjective that answers the question *whose.* (The answer is "their" in "their scientists.")

Day Five (optional): Creative Writing *Student page 65*

Pull out Student page 65. Write the student's name and the date for him as he watches, or ask him to write the name and date independently.

Instructor: Listen to the description of the Mongols one more time:

The Mongols came from the wild, cold mountains north of China. They lived in felt tents which they took down each morning, leaving nothing but ashes from their campfires behind. They were nomads who swept over the countryside, conquering and killing. The bone-chilling cold of the north didn't stop them; they wore furs and leather and rubbed their skin with grease to keep the wind away. They never settled down and grew crops; instead they ate foxes, rabbits, and other small wild creatures. But they could go without food for days at a time. If they were in danger of starving, they would open the veins of their horses, drink some blood, and then close the vein and ride on.

If you lived in ancient China, would you rather be a farmer settled in one place or a Mongol nomad, roving the steppes? What is one advantage of your choice? If you like, draw a picture of yourself as either a farmer or a Mongol.

WEEK 8

Day One: Narration Exercise *Student pages 67–69*

Focus: *Identifying the central narrative thread in a passage*

Pull out Student pages 67–68 and 69. Ask the student to write his name and the date on Student page 69.

Allow the student to read the story on Student pages 67–68, either silently or aloud.

Help the student begin to identify the central elements in the narrative by asking the following questions. He should try to answer these questions without looking back at the story, but if he cannot remember an answer after thinking for a few minutes, allow him to reread. Remind him to answer in complete sentences.

Instructor: What did Lucy see inside the wardrobe?
Student: *She saw long fur coats.*

Instructor: Why did she get into the wardrobe?
Student: *She liked the smell and the feel of fur OR She wanted to rub her face against the fur.*

Instructor: As she pushed towards the back of the wardrobe, what sound did she hear under her feet?
Student: *She heard crunching under her feet.*

Instructor: What did she think it was?
Student: *She thought it was moth-balls.*

Instructor: What did she feel rubbing against her face and hands instead of soft fur?
Student: *She felt something rough and prickly OR She felt branches.*

Instructor: When she came out of the back of the wardrobe, where was she?
Student: *She was standing in the middle of a wood.*

Instructor: What time was it?
Student: *It was night-time.*

Instructor: What did she see falling through the air?
Student: *She saw snow falling through the air.*

Instructor: How did Lucy feel?
Student: *She felt frightened, inquisitive, and excited.*

Instructor: What could she see behind her?
Student: *She could see the open door of the wardrobe OR She could see the room where the wardrobe was.*

Instructor: What did she do instead of going back?
Student: *She began to walk forward OR She began to walk towards the light.*

Now ask the student the general question, "Can you give me a brief summary of this passage?" The student should answer by summarizing the forward movement of the story, rather than listing details. His answer should be no more than three sentences and should resemble one of the following:

> "Lucy got into the wardrobe to feel the fur coats. As she pushed her way towards the back of the wardrobe, the soft fur turned to hard branches. She came out of the wardrobe into a little wood in the middle of the night."
>
> "Lucy pushed her way towards the back of the wardrobe. The fur turned into branches, and she came out into a little wood where it was snowing. When she looked behind her, she could see the room through the door of the wardrobe."
>
> "Lucy got into the wardrobe, but she discovered that the wardrobe was actually a door into a little wood. It was snowing and dark in the wood, and she could see a light. She decided to walk forward towards the light."

The student will probably attempt to put too much information into the summary. If he has difficulty condensing the story, ask the following three questions:

> Why did Lucy get into the wardrobe?
>
> What did she find at the back of the wardrobe?
>
> What did she do next?

Then have the student repeat his answers in order; this will form his brief summary.

Write down the student's narration on Student page 69 as he watches. When done, set the workbook page aside for the next lesson, which is on the back of it.

DAY TWO: Dictation Exercise *Student page 70*

Focus: *Adverbs that tell how, when, where, and how often*

Pull out Student page 70. Ask the student to write his name and the date.

Tell the student that today's dictation sentence comes from a little later in *The Lion, the Witch and the Wardrobe*. This time, when Lucy gets into the wardrobe, she shuts the door all the way.

Dictate the following sentence to the student two times. Pause at the comma, but don't tell the student ahead of time that the comma is there; give him a chance to put it in on his own.

> She shut the wardrobe door tightly behind her and looked around, panting for breath.

Ask the student to repeat the sentence back to you before he writes. If he cannot remember the entire sentence, you may repeat it additional times.

Watch the student as he writes, and correct him at once if he begins to make a mistake. When he is finished, tell him that this sentence has two adverbs in it. An adverb is a word that answers the questions "how, when, where, how often?" Tell him to underline the adverb "tightly." Ask the student what question this adverb answers. (It answers the question "how?" How did Lucy shut the door? She shut the door tightly.) Now tell him to underline the adverb "around." Ask the student what question this adverb answers. (It answers the question "where?" Where did Lucy look? She looked around.)

Day Three: Narration and Dictation *Student pages 71–73*

***Focus:** Identifying the central details in a description and writing original sentences from dictation*

Pull out Student pages 71–72 and 73. Ask the student to write his name and the date on Student page 73.

Today's exercise will combine narration and dictation. Allow the student to read the story on Student pages 71–72, either silently or aloud.

Help the student begin to identify the central details in the narrative by asking the following questions. He should try to answer these questions without looking back at the story, but if he cannot remember an answer after thinking for a few minutes, allow him to reread. Remind him to answer in complete sentences.

Instructor: Can you list three of the six things that the girls helped Mrs. Beaver to do in the very first sentence of the passage?
Student: *The girls helped Mrs. Beaver fill the kettle, lay the table, cut the bread, put the plates in the oven, draw a jug of beer, and put on the frying pan.*

Instructor: Why did they put plates in the oven?
Student: *They put plates in the oven to heat.*

Instructor: What was missing from the walls?
Student: *There were no books or pictures.*

Instructor: What did the beavers have instead of beds?
Student: *They had bunks built into the wall.*

Instructor: What two things were hanging from the roof?
Student: *Hams and strings of onions were hanging from the roof.*

Instructor: Name five of the ten things against the walls.
Student: *There were gum boots, oilskins, hatchets, shears, spades, trowels, things for carrying mortar, fishing rods, fishing nets, and sacks against the walls.*

Instructor: What did Mr. Beaver and Peter bring for the meal?
Student: *They brought fresh fish.*

Instructor: The children and the beavers had four things in their dinner. What were they?
Student: *They had fish, potatoes, milk (Mr. Beaver had beer), and butter.*

Instructor: What two things did they have for dessert?
Student: *They had marmalade roll and tea.*

Instructor: What did they sit on?
Student: *They sat on three-legged stools.*

Now ask the student the general question, "Can you give me a brief summary of this passage?" The student should answer with two sets of details: one about the house and one about the meal. His answer should be no more than three sentences and should resemble one of the following:

> "The beavers lived in a little home with bunks, but with no pictures on the walls. Instead they had hams hanging from the ceiling and all sorts of tools leaning against the walls. For dinner, the children and the beavers ate fish and potatoes, with marmalade roll for dessert."

> "The girls helped Mrs. Beaver get ready for dinner while Peter helped Mr. Beaver fish. The beavers' home had boots, hatchets, fishing nets, and sacks leaning against the wall. They all sat on three-legged stools and ate fish and potatoes for dinner."

> "The girls warmed plates, cut bread, and set the table for dinner. The cloth on the table was very rough, and they only had three-legged stools to sit on. The dinner was fish, potatoes, creamy milk, butter, and a marmalade roll for dessert."

If the student has difficulty summarizing the passage, ask him the following three questions:

> What did the house look like?
>
> What did the girls do to get ready for the meal?
>
> What did the beavers and the children eat for dinner?

The student's answers will serve as his narration.
Write down the student's narration on the lines below, but do not allow him to watch.

____

____

____

____

Then choose one or two sentences (about 12–15 words) to dictate back to the student. Repeat the sentences twice and ask the student to repeat them back to you before he writes on Student page 73. If he cannot repeat the sentences, read them again until he is able to keep them in mind.

Give all necessary help in spelling and punctuation.

When done, set the workbook page aside for the next lesson, which is on the back of it.

Day Four: Dictation Exercise *Student page 74*

Focus: *Adverbs that tell how, when, where, how often, to what extent*

Pull out Student page 74. Ask the student to write his name and the date.

Tell the student that today's dictation sentence comes from a little later in *The Lion, the Witch and the Wardrobe*. The children and the beavers set out on a journey and travel until they are very weary.

Dictate the following sentence to the student two times.

> Everyone was feeling very tired and very hungry when suddenly the trees began to get thinner in front of them and the ground to fall steeply downhill.

Ask the student to repeat the sentence back to you before he writes. If he cannot remember the entire sentence, you may repeat it additional times.

Watch the student as he writes, and correct him at once if he begins to make a mistake. When he is finished, tell him that this sentence has four adverbs in it. Remind him that an adverb is a word that answers the questions "how, when, where, how often?"

Tell him to underline the two adverbs "very." Tell the student that "very" answers another adverb question: "to what extent?" To what extent were the children tired? They were *very* tired. To what extent were the children hungry? They were *very* hungry. These adverbs modify the adjectives "tired" and "hungry."

Now tell the student to underline the adverb "suddenly." Ask the student what question this adverb answers. (It answers the question "how?" How did the trees get thinner? They got thinner *suddenly*. If the student answers "when," you may accept this as a valid answer.)

Finally, tell the student to underline the adverb *steeply*. Ask the student what question this adverb answers. (It answers the question "how?" How did the ground fall downhill? It fell *steeply* downhill. If the student answers "to what extent," you may accept this as a valid answer.)

Day Five (optional): Creative Writing *Student page 75*

Pull out Student page 75. Write the student's name and the date for her as she watches, or ask her to write the name and date independently.

> **Instructor:** In the story, Lucy walks through a wardrobe to a fantasy land called Narnia. If you could put a portal to Narnia in your room, where would you hide it? If you like, draw a picture of the portal in your room.

WEEK 9

Day One: Narration Exercise *Student pages 77–79*

Focus: *Identifying the central narrative thread in a passage*

Pull out Student pages 77–78 and 79. Ask the student to write her name and the date on Student page 79.

Allow the student to read the story on Student pages 77–78, either silently or aloud. This selection is a little more difficult than other passages, and some students may need you to read it out loud.

Help the student begin to identify the central elements in the narrative by asking the following questions. She should try to answer these questions without looking back at the story, but if she cannot remember an answer after thinking for a few minutes, allow her to reread. Remind her to answer in complete sentences.

Instructor: Why didn't C. S. Lewis apply to be exempt from the draft?
Student: *He thought it would be dishonorable.*

Instructor: What did he do while he was in the officers' training corps?
Student: *He worked on a collection of poems.*

Instructor: What country was he sent to fight in?
Student: *He was sent to France.*

Instructor: What message was Lewis trying to give his father, in his letters home?
Student: *He was trying to tell his father that he was safe.*

Instructor: What happened to Lewis during the Battle of Arras in France?
Student: *Lewis was wounded.*

Instructor: What did the doctors discover when Lewis was taken to the hospital?
Student: *He had a wound in his chest* **OR** *He was wounded and put out of combat permanently.*

Now ask the student the general question, "Can you give me a brief summary of this passage?" The student should answer by summarizing the progression of the narrative, rather than listing details. Her answer should be no more than three sentences and should resemble one of the following:

"C. S. Lewis decided not to get out of the draft. Instead he was sent to fight in France. He was wounded in a battle and was put out of combat."

"Jack was sent to France to fight for England. He wrote letters to his father telling his father that he was safe. But he was wounded in a battle and no longer had to fight."

"C. S. Lewis trained to be a soldier in the officers' training corps and then went to fight in France. He told his father that he was not in danger. Then he was wounded in the chest during a battle and could no longer fight."

The student will probably attempt to put too much information into the summary. If she has difficulty condensing the story, ask the following three questions:

What did C. S. Lewis do, against his father's wishes?

What did he tell his father in his letters?

What happened to him that made him leave the army?

Then have the student repeat her answers in order; this will form her brief summary.

Write down the student's narration on Student page 79 as she watches.

When done, set the workbook page aside for the next lesson, which is on the back of it.

Day Two: Dictation Exercise *Student page 80*

Focus: *Adverbs that tell how, when, where, how often, to what extent*

Pull out Student page 80. Ask the student to write her name and the date.

Tell the student that today's dictation sentence is from *A Child's Story of America* by three authors: Michael J. McHugh, Charles Morris, and Edward J. Shewan.

Dictate the following sentence to the student two times. Before you read, tell the student that "World War I" is a proper name and should be capitalized. You may need to explain that "I" is a Roman numeral (a number used by the Romans in ancient times) and means the same thing as "one" or "1." Be sure to indicate the question with your voice.

> Did you know that World War I was the most terrible war the world had ever seen up to that time?

Now ask the student to repeat the sentence back to you before she writes. Ask her to tell you what punctuation mark comes at the end. If she cannot remember the entire sentence, you may repeat it additional times.

Watch the student as she writes, and correct her at once if she begins to make a mistake. When she is finished, tell her to underline the word "most." This is an adverb. It answers the question "to what extent?" Ask the student to identify the word that "most" modifies. (The answer is "terrible." To what extent was the war terrible? It was *most* terrible.)

Now ask the student to underline the adverb "ever." Tell her that this adverb answers the question "when?"

Day Three: Narration and Dictation *Student pages 81–83*

Focus: *Identifying the central theme in a selection*

Pull out Student pages 81–82 and 83. Ask the student to write her name and the date on Student page 83.

Allow the student to read the story on Student pages 81–82, either silently or aloud. This selection is a little more difficult than other passages, and some students may need you to read it out loud.

Help the student begin to identify the central theme in the selection by asking the following questions. She should try to answer these questions without looking back at the story, but if she cannot remember an answer after thinking for a few minutes, allow her to reread. Remind her to answer in complete sentences.

Instructor: Were Germany and Russia on the same side, or on different sides?
Student: *Germany and Russia were on different sides.*

Instructor: How long did the Germans think that World War I would last?
Student: *The Germans thought the war would last four months.*

Instructor: The king of Germany, Kaiser Wilhelm II, told his troops that they would be home before what happened?
Student: *He told them they would be home before the leaves fell.*

Instructor: What did young men rush to do?
Student: *They rushed to join the army.*

Instructor: How long did most Russians think that the war would last?
Student: *They thought it would last two or three months.*

Instructor: What did the Imperial Guard officer want to pack, and why?
Student: *He wanted to pack his uniform so that he could wear it into Berlin.*

Now say to the student, "Try to tell me, in one sentence, what the Germans and Russians thought about the war." The student should respond, "The Germans and Russians thought the war would be over soon," OR "The Germans and Russians thought that the war would only last a few months," OR "The Germans and Russians were eager to fight because both sides expected to win easily." Prompt the student, if she seems uncertain, by asking the first and fifth comprehension questions again.

Once the student has come up with this sentence, say, "Now give me two more sentences with specific details in them about how each side felt." The purpose of this exercise is to guide the student into stating the central theme of the passage and supporting that theme with specifics.

The answer should resemble one of the following:

> "The Germans and Russians thought the war would be over soon. The Germans expected the war to last four months. The Russians thought it would only last two or three months."

> "The Germans and Russians thought that the war would only last a few months. The German king told his troops that they would be home before the leaves fell. One Russian officer packed his full-dress uniform so that he would be ready for victory."
>
> "The Germans and Russians were eager to fight because both sides expected to win easily. German soldiers wrote 'On to Paris' on the sides of their trains and expected to be in France in weeks. Russians thought they would win in two or three months."

Write down the student's narration on the lines below, but do not allow her to watch.

____

____

____

____

Then choose one or two sentences (about 12–15 words) to dictate back to the student. Repeat the sentences twice and ask the student to repeat them back to you before she writes on Student page 83. If she cannot repeat the sentences, read them again until she is able to keep them in mind.

Give all necessary help in spelling and punctuation.

When done, set the workbook page aside for the next lesson, which is on the back of it.

Day Four: Dictation Exercise *Student page 84*

Focus: *Adverbs that tell how, when, where, how often, to what extent*

Pull out Student page 84. Ask the student to write her name and the date.

Tell the student that today's dictation sentence is from the book *Everyday Life: World War I* by Walter A. Hazen.

Dictate the following sentence to the student two times.

> All nations now readied their armies for what they thought would be a brief war.

Ask the student to repeat the sentence back to you before she writes. If she cannot remember the sentence, you may repeat it additional times.

Watch the student as she writes, and correct her at once if she begins to make a mistake. When she is finished, tell her to underline the adverb "now." Ask the student what question this adverb answers. (The answer is "when?" When did the nations ready their armies? They readied the armies *now*.)

DAY FIVE (optional): Creative Writing *Student page 85*

Pull out Student page 85. Write the student's name and the date for him as he watches, or ask him to write the name and date independently.

> **Instructor:** Compose a short letter to someone you know who lives far away. You can compose the letter verbally while your parent or instructor writes down what you say. Tell your friend or relative what you have been up to lately. Write down either the first or last sentence of the letter by yourself and be sure to sign your name at the bottom.

WEEK 10

Day One: Narration Exercise *Student pages 87–89*

***Focus:** Identifying the central details in a passage*

Pull out Student pages 87–88 and 89. Ask the student to write his name and the date on Student page 89.

Allow the student to read the story on Student pages 87–88, either silently or aloud.

Help the student begin to identify the central details in the narrative by asking the following questions. He should try to answer these questions without looking back at the story, but if he cannot remember an answer after thinking for a few minutes, allow him to reread. Remind him to answer in complete sentences.

Instructor: There were two kinds of horses in the Horse-Barn. What were they?
Student: *Three-year-old colts and sedate work-horses were in the barn.*

Instructor: The three-year-old colts had soft noses. How soft were they?
Student: *They were as soft as velvet.*

Instructor: Could Almanzo stroke the soft noses of the colts?
Student: *No, he was not allowed to touch them.*

Instructor: What could a boy do to ruin a young horse?
Student: *He could scare it OR He could tease it OR He could strike it OR He could teach it to hate people.*

Instructor: Would Almanzo have done any of those things?
Student: *No, he would not.*

Instructor: What did Almanzo and Royal have to do to the stalls?
Student: *They had to clean out the soiled hay and spread fresh hay.*

Instructor: Which animals did Almanzo own?
Student: *He owned two calves.*

Instructor: What color were they?
Student: *The calves were red.*

Instructor: What did he name them? Why?
Student: *He named one Star, because of the white spot on his forehead. He named the other Bright because he was bright red all over.*

Instructor: What did the calves do when Almanzo scratched around their horns?
Student: *They licked him with their rough tongues.*

Now ask the student the general question, "Can you give me a brief summary of this passage?" The student should answer by listing details about the animals (the horses and calves) and about Almanzo's duties at the barn. His answer should be no more than three sentences and should resemble one of the following:

> "Almanzo had to clean out the stalls where the horses, cows, and sheep lived. He loved to see the colts, but he was not allowed to touch them. He had two calves of his own named Star and Bright."
>
> "Almanzo went to the barn every day after school. He had to take care of his two red calves, Star and Bright. He wanted to take care of the colts, but his father wouldn't let him."
>
> "Almanzo loved the colts, but he was not allowed to touch them or clean their stalls. Instead he helped his brother clean out the other stalls. Then he took care of his own two calves, who were named Star and Bright."

If the student has difficulty keeping the narration to three sentences, ask him the following three questions:

> How did Almanzo feel about the horses?
>
> What did Almanzo and Royal do to the stalls?
>
> Which animals belonged to Almanzo?

Have the student repeat his answers in order; this will form his brief summary.

Write down the student's narration on Student page 89 as he watches.

When done, set the workbook page aside for the next lesson, which is on the back of it.

Day Two: Dictation Exercise — *Student page 90*

***Focus:** Adverbs that tell how, when, where, how often, to what extent*

Pull out Student page 90. Ask the student to write his name and the date.

Tell the student that today's dictation sentence is from *Farmer Boy* and describes the barn.

Dictate the following sentence to the student two times. Before you read, tell the student that the last word of the sentence is actually two words linked together with a hyphen. Do not tell the student that the sentence contains a comma, but pause significantly when you reach it.

> The haymows were warm with the warmth of all the stock below, and the hay smelled dusty-sweet.

Now ask the student to repeat the sentence back to you before he writes. If he cannot remember the entire sentence, you may repeat it additional times.

Watch the student as he writes, and correct him at once if he begins to make a mistake or leaves out the comma. When he is finished, ask him to underline the adverb "below." Ask him which question this adverb answers. (The correct answer is "where?" Where is the stock? The stock is *below.*)

Day Three: Narration and Dictation *Student pages 91–93*

Focus: *Identifying the central details in a passage and writing original sentences from dictation*

Pull out Student pages 91–92 and 93. Ask the student to write his name and the date on Student page 93.

Today's exercise will combine narration and dictation. Allow the student to read the story on Student pages 91–92, either silently or aloud.

Help the student begin to identify the central details in the narrative by asking the following questions. He should try to answer these questions without looking back at the story, but if he cannot remember an answer after thinking for a few minutes, allow him to reread. Remind him to answer in complete sentences.

Instructor: Can you list four of the seven things that Almanzo saw on the table?
Student: *He saw cheese, headcheese, jams, jellies, preserves, milk, and baked beans with fat pork.*

Instructor: What kind of rug did Mother make for the dining-room?
Student: *She made a rug out of dyed rags.*

Instructor: Can you list two of the four things that sat in the corner cupboards?
Student: *Sea-shells, petrified wood, curious rocks, and books sat in the corner cupboards.*

Instructor: What hung over the center table? What was it made of?
Student: *An air-castle made of wheat straws hung over the center table.*

Instructor: What three words are used to describe Mother?
Student: *She is short, plump, and pretty.*

Instructor: What did Mother's hair look like?
Student: *It was brown and looked like a bird's smooth wings.*

Instructor: What color were her buttons and sleeves?
Student: *Her buttons and sleeves were red.*

Instructor: What was tied around her waist?
Student: *A white apron was tied around her waist.*

Instructor: Why did she have to tug her way through the door?
Student: *Her hoop-skirts were wider than the door.*

Instructor: Whose plate was filled first?
Student: *Mr. Corse's OR The schoolmaster's plate was filled first.*

Instructor: Whose plate was filled last?
Student: *Almanzo's plate was filled last.*

Instructor: Almanzo ate twelve different things! Can you list eight of them?
Student: *Almanzo ate baked beans, salt pork, potatoes with gravy, ham, bread and butter, mashed turnips, stewed yellow pumpkin, plum preserves, strawberry jam, grape jelly, watermelon-rind pickles, and pumpkin pie.*

Now tell the student to describe, in three sentences, either the dinner itself, Mother, or the dining-room. His answer should resemble one of the following:

> "When Almanzo came into the house, the ham, cheese, and baked beans smelled so good that he could hardly bear it. He was served last at dinner. But then he ate baked beans, potatoes with gravy, turnips, pumpkin, ham, pickles, and pumpkin pie."
>
> "The dining room in Almanzo's house had brown wallpaper and an air-castle hanging over the table. There were corner cupboards with interesting shells and books in them, and Almanzo's mother had made a rag rug for the floor."
>
> "Almanzo's mother had a hoop-skirt so wide that she had trouble getting through the door. She had smooth brown hair, and her dress had red buttons and red sleeves. She was short and pretty."

Then have the student repeat his answers in order; this will form his brief summary. Write down the student's narration on the lines below, but do not allow him to watch.

____

____

____

____

Then choose one or two sentences (about 12–15 words) to dictate back to the student. Repeat the sentences twice and ask the student to repeat them back to you before he writes on Student page 93. If he cannot repeat the sentences, read them again until he is able to keep them in mind.

Give all necessary help in spelling and punctuation.

When done, set the workbook page aside for the next lesson, which is on the back of it.

Day Four: Dictation Exercise — *Student page 94*

Focus: *Adverbs that tell how, when, where, how often, to what extent*

Pull out Student page 94. Ask the student to write his name and the date.

Tell the student that today's dictation sentence is from *Farmer Boy* and describes Almanzo getting ready for bed after his huge dinner.

Dictate the following sentence to the student two times.

> The bedroom was so cold that he could hardly unbutton his clothes and put on his long woolen nightshirt and nightcap.

Now ask the student to repeat the sentence back to you before he writes. If he cannot remember the entire sentence, you may repeat it additional times.

Watch the student as he writes, and correct him at once if he begins to make a mistake. When he is finished, ask him to underline the adverb "so." Tell him that this adverb answers the question "to what extent?" To what extent was the bedroom cold? It was *so* cold.

Now ask the student to underline the adverb "hardly." Ask him which question this adverb answers. (The correct answer is "how?" How could he unbutton his clothes? He could *hardly* unbutton his clothes.)

DAY FIVE (optional): Creative Writing — *Student page 95*

Pull out Student page 95. Write the student's name and the date for her as she watches, or ask her to write the name and date independently.

> **Instructor:** What is your favorite food? Describe it by answering at least three of the following questions: What does it look like? What does it taste like? What does it smell like? What does it feel like? What does it sound like when you bite into it? If you like, draw a picture of your favorite food, using your description as a guide.

Remind the student to answer you in 1-2 complete sentences. If he answers in a fragment, turn the fragment into a complete sentence, say it to him, and then ask him to repeat this sentence back to you.

WEEK 11

DAY ONE: Narration Exercise *Student pages 97–98*

Focus: *Identifying the central narrative thread in a passage*

Pull out Student pages 97 and 98. Ask the student to write her name and the date on Student page 98.

Allow the student to read the story on Student page 97, either silently or aloud.

Help the student begin to identify the central elements in the narrative by asking the following questions. She should try to answer these questions without looking back at the story, but if she cannot remember an answer after thinking for a few minutes, allow her to reread. Remind her to answer in complete sentences.

Instructor: Who was Hor-em-heb?
Student: *He was the Master Builder.*

Instructor: After the doors to the treasure chamber were locked, what was put on them?
Student: *Pharaoh's seal was placed on them.*

Instructor: How did Hor-em-heb trick the Pharaoh?
Student: *He built a secret passage into the treasure chamber.*

Instructor: The story says that Hor-em-heb was "able to add to the reward which Pharaoh gave to him." What do you think this means?
Student: *He was stealing from the treasure chamber. [You may need to prompt the student for this answer.]*

Instructor: After Hor-em-heb died, who began to use the secret passage to steal treasure?
Student: *Hor-em-heb's two sons began to steal the treasure.*

Instructor: What did Pharaoh do when he found that his treasure was disappearing?
Student: *He set traps near the treasure.*

Instructor: Did the traps work?
Student: *Yes, one of the brothers was caught.*

Now ask the student the general question, "Can you give me a brief summary of this passage?" The student should answer by summarizing the plot, rather than listing details. Her answer should be no more than three sentences and should resemble one of the following:

> "The Pharaoh asked his Master Builder to build him a treasure room. The Master Builder made a secret passage into the treasure room. He and his sons stole the treasure."

"Hor-em-heb, who was the Pharaoh's Master Builder, made a treasure room with a secret passage. He used the passage to steal treasure. He told his sons about the passage before he died, and they used it to steal even more."

"The Master Builder built the Pharaoh a treasure room with a secret passage. He used the passage to steal treasure, and after he died his sons used it too. But the Pharaoh set traps and caught one of the sons."

If the student has trouble condensing the information in the passage, ask the following three questions:

What did Hor-em-heb do?

What did this allow him and his sons to do?

What did the Pharaoh do about it?

Then have the student repeat her answers in order; this will form her brief summary. Write down the student's narration on Student page 98 as she watches.

Day Two: Dictation Exercise *Student page 99*

***Focus:** Remembering dictation sentences after three repetitions*

Pull out Student page 99. Dictate the following sentences to the student three times. Before you read, tell the student that you will read the sentences only three times before asking her to write.

Also tell the student that in these sentences, "pharaoh" should not be capitalized because it does not stand for a particular person. It was capitalized in the story from "The Treasure Thief" because it named a particular pharaoh, Rameses III.

Indicate the period after the first sentence with your voice. You will probably need to remind the student that "pharaoh" is spelled with the *a* before the *o*.

> The king of Egypt was called the pharaoh. The pharaohs of Egypt built pyramids to protect their treasures and their graves.

Now ask the student to repeat the sentences back to you before she writes. If she forgets, tell her to go back to the beginning of the sentences and recite them again to jog her memory.

If necessary, you may then prompt the student with single words.

Watch the student as she writes, and correct her at once if she begins to make a mistake.

Day Three: Narration and Dictation *Student pages 101–102*

***Focus:** Identifying the central narrative thread in a passage and writing original sentences from dictation*

Pull out Student pages 101 and 102. Ask the student to write her name and the date on Student page 102.

Today's exercise will combine narration and dictation. Allow the student to read the story on Student page 101, either silently or aloud.

Help the student begin to identify the central elements in the narrative by asking the following questions. She should try to answer these questions without looking back at the story, but if she cannot remember an answer after thinking for a few minutes, allow her to reread. Remind her to answer in complete sentences.

Instructor: In this passage, the treasure chamber isn't built into a pyramid. What building is it part of?
Student: *It is part of the king's palace.*

Instructor: What kind of door did the builder put into the wall?
Student: *He put a stone in the wall that could be taken out.*

Instructor: To whom did the builder tell his secret?
Student: *He told it to his sons.*

Instructor: Why could the king not blame anyone for the thefts? Two reasons were given.
Student: *The seals on the door weren't broken, and the chamber was locked.*

Instructor: What did the king do to protect his treasure?
Student: *He put traps around the treasure.*

Instructor: What happened to the thieves?
Student: *One of them was caught in a trap.*

Now ask the student the general question, "Can you give me a brief summary of this passage?" The student should answer by summarizing the plot, rather than listing details. Her answer should be no more than three sentences and should resemble one of the following:

"The builder built a treasure room onto the king's palace, but he left a loose stone in the wall so that he could steal treasure. He told his sons about the stone before he died. His sons also stole treasure, but one of them got caught in a trap."

"The king told his builder to make a treasure room. The builder left a removable stone in the wall, so that he and his sons could steal the treasure. When the king realized that his treasure was disappearing, he set a trap and caught one of the thieves."

"The builder planned to make himself and his sons comfortable with the king's treasure. So he left a loose stone in the wall, so that they could always get into the treasure room. But the king set traps around the money, and one of the builder's sons was caught."

If she has trouble condensing the information in the passage, ask the following three questions:

What did the builder do to the treasure room?

Who stole the money?

How did the king respond to the disappearing money?

Then have the student repeat her answers in order; this will form her brief summary. Write down the student's narration on the lines below, but do not allow her to watch.

____

____

____

____

Then choose one or two sentences (about 15–18 words) to dictate back to the student. Repeat the sentences three times and ask the student to repeat them back to you before she writes on Student page 102.

Give all necessary help in spelling and punctuation.

Day Four: Dictation Exercise *Student page 103*

***Focus:** Remembering dictation sentences after three repetitions*

Pull out Student page 103. Ask the student to write her name and the date.

Dictate the following sentences to the student three times. Before you read, tell the student that you will read the sentences only three times before asking her to write, and will not repeat them afterwards. Tell the student that you will pause briefly for each comma, and for a longer time at the first period.

Now ask the student to repeat the sentences back to you before she writes. If she forgets, tell her to go back to the beginning of the sentences and recite them again to jog her memory.

If necessary, you may then prompt the student with single words.

> Roger Lancelyn Green retold the stories of the Egyptians. When he was younger, he studied at Oxford, where his tutor was C. S. Lewis.

Watch the student as she writes, and correct her at once if she begins to make a mistake. You may need to help her spell "Lancelyn." You may also need to explain that "C." and "S." are capitalized and that each is followed by a period, since those letters are abbreviations for Lewis's full name (Clive Staples).

When done, set the workbook page aside for the next lesson, which is on the back of it.

DAY FIVE (optional): Creative Writing

Student page 104

Pull out Student page 104. Write the student's name and the date for him as he watches, or ask him to write the name and date independently.

For creative writing activities for weeks 11-20, student responses to the prompt should be two sentences of roughly 15-18 words.

> **Instructor:** Imagine you have a treasure that you want to keep safe. Where would you put it?

WEEK 12

Day One: Narration Exercise *Student pages 105–107*

Focus: *Identifying the central narrative thread in a passage*

Pull out Student pages 105–106 and 107. Ask the student to write his name and the date on Student page 107.

Allow the student to read the story on Student pages 105–106, either silently or aloud.

Help the student begin to identify the central elements in the narrative by asking the following questions. He should try to answer these questions without looking back at the story, but if he cannot remember an answer after thinking for a few minutes, allow him to reread. Remind him to answer in complete sentences.

Instructor: How did Ali Baba earn his living?
Student: *He sold sticks at the market.*

Instructor: How did his brother Kasim earn a living?
Student: *He had a rich wife and sold carpets.*

Instructor: How did Ali Baba know that the men in the woods were robbers?
Student: *They were rough, used bad language, and had plunder on their horses.*

Instructor: What happened when the leader of the robbers shouted "Open sesame!"
Student: *The rock swung open and a cave appeared.*

Instructor: How did they close the door to the cave?
Student: *The leader shouted, "Close sesame!"*

Instructor: When Ali Baba went into the cave, what did he see?
Student: *He saw treasure OR He saw silver, gold, jewels, and carpets.*

Instructor: What did Ali Baba take home with him?
Student: *He took four bags of gold coins.*

Instructor: How did Ali Baba and his wife count the coins?
Student: *They borrowed a corn measure from his brother.*

Instructor: What did Kasim's wife do to the corn measure?
Student: *She put tar on the bottom of the measuring pail.*

Instructor: What did she find stuck to the tar when the corn measure was returned?
Student: *She found a gold coin.*

Now ask the student the general question, "Can you give me a brief summary of this passage?" The student should answer by summarizing the plot, rather than listing details. His answer should be no more than three sentences and should resemble one of the following:

"Ali Baba discovered a cave filled with treasure. He took gold coins home for his wife to count, but his brother's wife found out about the coins."

"Ali Baba was a poor man, but his brother was rich. By accident, Ali Baba found out where robbers were storing their gold. He tried to keep the gold a secret from his brother, but his brother's wife discovered the secret."

"Ali Baba was gathering sticks when he saw robbers storing their plunder in a cave. He took some of the coins home to his wife. They borrowed a corn measure from his brother's wife, but she put tar on the measure and a coin stuck to the tar."

The student will probably attempt to put too much information into the summary. If he has difficulty condensing the story, ask the following three questions:

What did Ali Baba discover?

How did he and his wife measure it?

How did Kasim's wife discover their secret?

Then have the student repeat his answers in order; this will form his brief summary.
Write down the student's narration on Student page 107 as he watches.
When done, set the workbook page aside for the next lesson, which is on the back of it.

Day Two: Dictation Exercise *Student page 108*

Focus: *Proper nouns*

Pull out Student page 108. Ask the student to write his name and the date.

Tell the student that today's dictation sentence is from "The First Voyage of Sinbad," another story in *The Thousand and One Nights*. Sinbad is beginning the story of his adventures.

Dictate the following sentences to the student three times. Before you read, tell the student that you will read the sentences only three times before asking him to write, and will not repeat them afterwards.

Tell the student that the selection has three sentences in it. There is also one comma. You will pause briefly at the comma, and for a longer time at each period.

> We left Baghdad at once. We set sail, and steered our course through the Persian Gulf. The Persian Gulf is formed by the coasts of Arabia on the right and Persia on the left.

Now ask the student to repeat the sentences back to you before he writes. If he forgets, tell him to go back to the beginning of the sentences and recite them again to jog his memory. If necessary, you may then prompt the student with single words.

Remind the student that there are four names, or proper nouns, in the selection: Baghdad, Persian Gulf, Arabia, and Persia. All of these should be capitalized.

Watch the student as he writes, and correct him at once if he begins to make a mistake.

Day Three: Narration and Dictation *Student pages 109–110*

***Focus:** Identifying the central narrative thread in a passage and writing original sentences from dictation*

Pull out Student page 109. Ask the student to write his name and the date on Student page 110.

Today's exercise will combine narration and dictation. Allow the student to read the story on Student page 109, either silently or aloud.

Help the student begin to identify the central elements in the narrative by asking the following questions. He should try to answer these questions without looking back at the story, but if he cannot remember an answer after thinking for a few minutes, allow him to reread. Remind him to answer in complete sentences.

Instructor: What did Kasim's wife do when she found the golden coin?
Student: *She told her husband about it.*

Instructor: Was Kasim pleased over Ali Baba's good luck?
Student: *No, he was jealous.*

Instructor: What did Ali Baba offer Kasim so that his brother would keep the secret?
Student: *He offered Kasim part of his treasure.*

Instructor: How many treasure chests did Kasim take with him to the cave?
Student: *He took ten chests.*

Instructor: After Kasim filled his treasure chests, he tried to get out. What did he say to the cave door?
Student: *He said, "Open, Barley."*

Instructor: Did the door open?
Student: *No, it did not.*

Now ask the student the general question, "Can you give me a brief summary of this passage?" The student should answer by summarizing the plot, rather than listing details. His answer should be no more than three sentences and should resemble one of the following:

> "Kasim's wife was jealous and told her husband about the gold. Kasim discovered Ali Baba's secret. He set off to the cave to take the treasure, but he forgot how to reopen the cave door."
>
> "Kasim learned about Ali Baba's wealth from his wife. Ali Baba told him how to get into the cave, and begged him to keep the secret. Kasim went to the cave alone, but once he was inside, he forgot the words 'Open, Sesame.'"
>
> "Kasim's wife told him all about Ali Baba's wealth. Then Kasim decided to take the treasure for himself. He went to the cave and opened the door, but once he was inside, he forgot how to open it so that he could get back out."

If he has difficulty condensing the story, ask the following three questions:

How did Kasim find out about the treasure?

What did he do?

What went wrong with his plan?

Then have the student repeat his answers in order; this will form his brief summary. Write down the student's narration on the lines below, but do not allow him to watch.

____

____

____

____

Then choose two or three sentences (15–18 words) to dictate back to the student. Repeat the sentences three times and ask the student to repeat them back to you before he writes on Student page 110.

Give all necessary help in spelling and punctuation.

Day Four: Dictation Exercise — *Student page 111*

Focus: *Proper nouns and names of books*

Pull out Student page 111. Ask the student to write his name and the date.

Tell the student that today's dictation sentence is from *The Story of the World: The Middle Ages.* This sentence is a little shorter because it has something new in it: the name of a book, *The Thousand and One Nights.*

Tell the student that when he writes the name of a book, he should capitalize the first word of the title and every other important word in the title. In *The Thousand and One Nights*, all of the words except for "and" are capitalized. Also, the names of books are usually put in italics. But when you are writing by hand, you underline the name of a book instead.

Dictate the following sentence to the student three times. Before you read, tell the student that you will read the sentence only three times before asking him to write, and will not repeat it afterwards. Also tell the student that there are two commas in the sentence, and that you will pause briefly at each one.

> One of the most famous Islamic books, The Thousand and One Nights, takes place in the palace of the caliph in Baghdad.

Now ask the student to repeat the sentence back to you before he writes. If he forgets, tell him to go back to the beginning of the sentence and recite it again to jog his memory. If necessary, you may then prompt the student with single words.

Remind the student that the sentence contains two other names besides *The Thousand and One Nights*: "Baghdad" and "Islamic." Both should be capitalized.

Watch the student as he writes, and correct him at once if he begins to make a mistake. When done, set the workbook page aside for the next lesson, which is on the back of it.

Day Five (optional): Creative Writing *Student page 112*

Pull out Student page 112. Write the student's name and the date for her as she watches, or ask her to write the name and date independently.

> **Instructor:** If you discovered a cave full of gold like Ali Baba, what is the first thing you would buy with your new wealth? If you like, draw a picture of the first thing you would buy.

WEEK 13

DAY ONE: Narration Exercise *Student pages 113–115*

***Focus:** Identifying the central details in a passage*

Pull out Student pages 113–114 and 115. Ask the student to write her name and the date on Student page 115.

Allow the student to read the story on Student pages 113–114, either silently or aloud.

Help the student begin to identify the central details in the narrative by asking the following questions. She should try to answer these questions without looking back at the story, but if she cannot remember an answer after thinking for a few minutes, allow her to reread. Remind her to answer in complete sentences.

Instructor: What is one thing that Oliver found in the first room?
Student: *He found an old bedspring, an empty barrel, and a jar with a large spider.*

Instructor: The second room was filled with treasures. What cave was it like?
Student: *It was like Ali Baba's cave.*

Instructor: What were the two sleds named?
Student: *They were named Snow Demon and Little Kriss Kringle.*

Instructor: What was unusual about the old bicycle?
Student: *The front wheel was very tall and the back wheel was small.*

Instructor: Can you remember three other things that Oliver found in the second room?
Student: *He found a tin bathtub, jars with spiders in them, a doll carriage, a coffee grinder, a crib frame, and books.*

Instructor: What covered all of the objects in the room?
Student: *A layer of white dust covered everything.*

Instructor: What did Oliver spend the rest of the afternoon doing?
Student: *He spent it reading old books OR old magazines.*

Instructor: What three things were missing from the world of the old books?
Student: *There were no cars, no airplanes, and no trains.*

Now ask the student the general question, "Can you give me a brief summary of this passage?" The student should answer by describing the room and what Oliver did there. Her answer should be no more than three sentences and should resemble one of the following:

> "Oliver found a room filled with treasures. It had sleds, an old bicycle, old toys, and old books, all covered with dust. He spent all afternoon reading the old books.

"Oliver found a treasure room with sleds, an old bicycle, a tin bathtub, and old books in it. The books were all about a time when there were no cars, planes, or trains."

"Oliver spent all afternoon reading in a secret room. He found the room while he was exploring. It was like a treasure room, filled with things like sleds, an old bike, a bathtub painted blue, old books, and a doll carriage."

Write down the student's narration on Student page 115 as she watches.
When done, set the workbook page aside for the next lesson, which is on the back of it.

Day Two: Dictation Exercise *Student page 116*

***Focus:** Helping verbs and direct quotations*

Pull out Student page 116. Ask the student to write her name and the date.

Tell the student that today's dictation sentence is also from *The Four-Story Mistake.* This sentence is a little shorter because it has something new in it: a direct quotation.

Tell the student that a direct quotation is the exact words that someone speaks. In this sentence, Cuffy says Oliver's name twice. The student should put quotation marks around these names to show that Cuffy says them.

Show the student the dictation sentences. Point to the quotation marks. Show the student that the quotation marks go right at the beginning of Cuffy's words, and after the punctuation mark that *ends* Cuffy's words. The first word after that, "cried," does not begin with a capital letter because Cuffy's words are *part* of the sentence. This is not the end of the sentence, even though there is an exclamation point after "Oliver! Oliver!"

Now take the book away and dictate the following sentences to the student three times. Before you read, tell the student that you will read the sentence only three times before asking her to write, and will not repeat it afterwards. Be sure to use a different voice for "Oliver! Oliver!" to indicate that these are Cuffy's exact words.

> Hours later his reluctant ear was pierced by the frantically repeated sound of his name. "Oliver! Oliver!" cried Cuffy.

Now ask the student to repeat the sentences back to you before she writes. If she forgets, tell her to go back to the beginning of the sentences and recite them again to jog her memory. If necessary, you may then prompt the student with single words.

Watch the student as she writes, and correct her at once if she begins to make a mistake in either spelling or punctuation. You may need to remind her that there is an exclamation point after each "Oliver!"

When she is finished, tell her to underline the verb "was pierced." Tell her that "pierced" is an action verb and "was" is a helping verb. It would sound silly to say, "His reluctant ear pierced." "Was" has to help out the verb "pierced."

Day Three: Narration and Dictation *Student pages 117–119*

***Focus:** Identifying the central details in a passage and writing original sentences from dictation*

Pull out Student pages 117–118 and 119. Ask the student to write her name and the date on Student page 119.

Today's exercise will combine narration and dictation. Allow the student to read the story on Student pages 117–118, either silently or aloud.

Help the student begin to identify the central details in the narrative by asking the following questions. She should try to answer these questions without looking back at the story, but if she cannot remember an answer after thinking for a few minutes, allow her to reread. Remind her to answer in complete sentences.

Instructor: What did the children use for sliding down the hill after they tried the sleds?
Student: *They slid down the hill on dishpans.*

Instructor: Which child didn't like the dishpans?
Student: *Oliver didn't like the spinning.*

Instructor: What did they decide to do next?
Student: *They made snow ice cream.*

Instructor: What two ingredients did they get from Cuffy for the ice cream?
Student: *They got milk and sugar.*

Instructor: How did Oliver react to the snow ice cream?
Student: *He ate so much that his stomach felt strange.*

Instructor: After the other three had gone to the house, what did Rush do?
Student: *He went for a walk in the snow.*

Instructor: Who went with him?
Student: *The dog Isaac went with him.*

Instructor: The story draws a contrast between the snowy woods and the house. A contrast is when the differences between two things are pointed out. What two words describe the woods?
Student: *The woods are beautiful and mysterious.*

Instructor: What three things does Rush suddenly long for?
Student: *He longs for noise, warmth, and light.*

Instructor: How are the windows of the kitchen described?
Student: *They are bright.*

Now ask the student the general question, "Can you give me a brief summary of this passage?" The student should answer by describing three things: the sledding, the ice cream, and the walk in the woods. Her answer should be no more than three sentences and should resemble one of the following:

> "The children slid down the hill on dishpans that went around and around and made Oliver sick. Then they made snow ice cream, and Oliver ate so much that his stomach felt strange. Then Rush went for a walk in the woods, but he got cold and headed back to the house."
>
> "The children went sledding on sleds and dishpans. Then they made snow ice cream with milk and sugar. Rush took his dog for a walk in the woods, but he decided to go back to where there was light and noise."
>
> "The children sledded on dishpans and made ice cream from snow, milk, and sugar. Then Rush decided to go for a walk in the woods with his dog Isaac. The woods were beautiful and mysterious, but he got cold and wanted to go back to the warm bright kitchen."

Write down the student's narration on the lines below, but do not allow her to watch.

____

____

____

____

Then choose two or three sentences (15–18 words) to dictate back to the student. Repeat the sentences three times and ask the student to repeat them back to you before she writes on Student page 119.

Give all necessary help in spelling and punctuation.

When done, set the workbook page aside for the next lesson, which is on the back of it.

Day Four: Dictation Exercise *Student page 120*

***Focus:** Helping verbs and semicolons*

Pull out Student page 120. Ask the student to write her name and the date.

Tell the student that today's dictation sentence is from *The Four-Story Mistake*. It describes how the snow looks to the children as it falls.

Dictate the following sentence to the student three times. Before you read, tell the student that you will read the sentence only three times before asking her to write, and will not repeat it afterwards.

Tell the student that there is one comma and one semicolon in the sentence. The semicolon separates two complete sentences and takes the place of a period. Tell the student that you will pause briefly at the comma and for a longer time at the semicolon.

> By lunchtime the valley was lightly coated, like a cake with confectioner's sugar; and by half past three the snow was of a respectable depth.

Now ask the student to repeat the sentence back to you before she writes. Remind her that "confectioner's" is a possessive and has an apostrophe before the *s*. If she forgets part of the sentence, tell her to go back to the beginning of the sentence and recite it again to jog her memory.

If necessary, you may then prompt the student with single words.

Watch the student as she writes, and correct her at once if she begins to make a mistake. You may need to help her spell "confectioner's."

When she is finished, tell her to underline the verbs "was" and "coated" on the first line, and "was" on the second line. Tell her that "coated" is an action verb and "was" is a helping verb. It would sound silly to say, "The valley lightly coated." "Was" has to help out the verb "coated."

Point out that the "was" on the second line is a state of being verb that stands alone. It does not help out an action verb. "Was" can be either a state of being *or* a helping verb.

Day Five (optional): Creative Writing *Student page 121*

Pull out Student page 121. Write the student's name and the date for him as he watches, or ask him to write the name and date independently.

> **Instructor:** The Melendy family lives in a house with four stories. Imagine you could talk to your house. What would it sound like? Does it have an old voice or a young voice? Does it have a big deep voice or a small high voice? If you like, draw a picture of your house. You could even give your house eyes and a mouth.

WEEK 14

Day One: Narration Exercise *Student pages 123–125*

***Focus:** Identifying the central narrative thread in a passage*

Pull out Student pages 123-124 and 125. Ask the student to write his name and the date on Student page 125.

Allow the student to read the story on Student pages 123–124, either silently or aloud.

Help the student begin to identify the central elements in the narrative by asking the following questions. He should try to answer these questions without looking back at the story, but if he cannot remember an answer after thinking for a few minutes, allow him to reread. Remind him to answer in complete sentences.

Instructor: Why was one kitten named Mask?
Student: *It was a black kitten with a white face.*

Instructor: Why was another kitten named Funny?
Student: *She had one green eye and one blue eye.*

Instructor: What were the rules of the kitten-choosing game? Be sure you tell me what part the hat, the names on four pieces of paper, the four corners of the room, and the kittens play in the game.
Student: *The kittens' names were written on pieces of paper put into a hat. Rufus drew the names out of the hat. Each kitten was placed in the middle of the room. The four children went to the four corners of the room and called "Kitty, kitty."*

Instructor: What kitten was first to be chosen?
Student: *Funny was the first.*

Instructor: Which child ended up with Funny?
Student: *Sylvie ended up with Funny.*

Instructor: When Whiskers was placed in the center of the room, what did he do?
Student: *He just sat there.*

Instructor: What did the children have to do to get him to play?
Student: *They had to get right up next to him.*

Instructor: Who ended up with Whiskers?
Student: *Rufus got Whiskers.*

Now ask the student the general question, "Can you give me a brief summary of this passage?" The student should answer by summarizing the choosing game, rather than listing details. His answer should be no more than three sentences and should resemble one of the following:

"The four Moffats played a game to choose their kittens. They placed each kitten in the center of the room and called 'Here, kitty, kitty!' Whichever person the kitten went to became the owner of that kitten."

"The Moffats put the names of the kittens on pieces of paper and drew them out of a hat. Each kitten was placed in the center of the room. The children called, 'Here, kitty, kitty!' and tried to get the kitten to come."

"The Moffat children placed each kitten in the middle of the room. They went to the four corners of the room and called the kittens. Funny went to Sylvie, and Whiskers went to Rufus, so they were out of the game."

If he has difficulty condensing the game into three sentences, ask the following three questions:

Where did the children stand?

Where were the kittens put?

What did the children try to get the kittens to do?

Then have the student repeat his answers in order; this will form his brief summary.

Write down the student's narration on Student page 125 as he watches.

When done, set the workbook page aside for the next lesson, which is on the back of it.

Day Two: Dictation Exercise *Student page 126*

***Focus:** Direct objects following action verbs*

Pull out Student page 126. Ask the student to write his name and the date.

Tell the student that today's dictation sentences are also from *The Moffats.* In these sentences, Jane is watching her mother cook apples for apple pie.

Dictate the following sentences to the student three times. Before you read, tell the student that you will read the sentences only three times before asking him to write, and will not repeat them afterwards.

> She set the blue and white kettle of apples on the stove. She sprinkled sugar and cinnamon on the apples with the same deft fingers.

Now ask the student to repeat the sentences back to you before he writes. If he forgets, tell him to go back to the beginning of the sentences and recite them again to jog his memory. If necessary, you may then prompt the student with single words.

Watch the student as he writes, and correct him at once if he begins to make a mistake. When he is finished, tell him to underline the action verbs "set" and "sprinkled." Ask the student, "Set what?" He should answer "kettle." (If he answers "blue and white kettle of apples," ask him which *one* word represents the thing which is "set.") Tell him that "kettle" is the *direct object* of the verb "set." What did Jane's mother set on the stove? She set the kettle. The kettle "receives" the action of the verb *set.* Tell him to write the initials "d.o." over the word "kettle."

Now ask the student, "Sprinkled what?" He should answer "sugar and cinnamon." Tell him that "sugar" and "cinnamon" are both direct objects of the verb "sprinkled." What did Jane's mother sprinkle? She sprinkled sugar and cinnamon. Sugar and cinnamon both "receive" the action of the verb *sprinkled.* Tell him to write the initials "d.o." over the word "sugar" and also over the word "cinnamon."

Day Three: Narration and Dictation *Student pages 127–129*

Focus: *Identifying the central narrative thread in a passage and writing original sentences from dictation*

Pull out Student pages 127–128 and 129. Ask the student to write his name and the date on Student page 129.

Today's exercise will combine narration and dictation. Allow the student to read the story on Student pages 127–128, either silently or aloud.

Help the student begin to identify the central elements in the narrative by asking the following questions. He should try to answer these questions without looking back at the story, but if he cannot remember an answer after thinking for a few minutes, allow him to reread. Remind him to answer in complete sentences.

Instructor: What was Boots doing while the game was going on?
Student: *She was clawing at the box and meowing to get out.*

Instructor: What did she do as soon as she was set on the floor?
Student: *She raced madly around and whacked a tassel.*

Instructor: Whom did Jane think Boots would choose?
Student: *She thought Boots would choose Joey.*

Instructor: What did Boots suddenly do?
Student: *She jumped into Jane's lap.*

Instructor: Which kitten went to Joey?
Student: *Mask went to Joey.*

Instructor: What did Joey find to be unusual about Mask? The story lists four things.
Student: *Mask had the longest fur, the prettiest markings, and the longest tail. He was also smallest.*

Instructor: What did Jane do with Boots when the game was over?
Student: *She put Boots back in the box with her mother.*

Now ask the student the general question, "Can you give me a brief summary of this passage?" The student should answer by summarizing the plot, rather than listing details. His answer should be no more than three sentences and should resemble one of the following:

> "Jane and Joe both wanted Boots. At first Jane thought that Boots would choose Joe, but then Boots jumped into her lap. Joey got Mask instead."
>
> "Jane wanted to own Boots, even though she thought she didn't deserve to. But Boots jumped in her lap and Mask went to Joey. Joey decided that Mask had the longest fur, the prettiest markings, and the longest tail."
>
> "Boots was the most energetic of all the kittens. Jane wanted her more than anything in the world. She thought that Boots would go to Joey, but then Boots jumped into her lap and became hers."

If he has difficulty condensing the story, ask the following three questions:

> What did Jane want?
>
> What did Jane get, and how?
>
> What did Joey get, and how did he feel about it?

Then have the student repeat his answers in order; this will form his brief summary. Write down the student's narration on the lines below, but do not allow him to watch.

____

____

____

____

Then choose two or three sentences (15–18 words) to dictate back to the student. Repeat the sentences three times and ask the student to repeat them back to you before he writes on Student page 129.

Give all necessary help in spelling and punctuation.

When done, set the workbook page aside for the next lesson, which is on the back of it.

Day Four: Dictation Exercise *Student page 130*

Focus: *Direct objects following action verbs*

Pull out Student page 130. Ask the student to write his name and the date.

Tell the student that today's dictation sentences are also from *The Moffats.* This happens *before* the choosing game begins.

Dictate the following sentences to the student three times. Before you read, tell the student that you will read the sentences only three times before asking him to write, and will not repeat them afterwards.

Tell him that there are two sentences. One ends with a period and one ends with an exclamation point. When you read, be sure to indicate the exclamation point with your voice.

> Jane clutched the nickel tightly in her fist and walked slowly up the street. Think of all the fine things it might buy!

Now ask the student to repeat the sentences back to you before he writes. If he forgets, tell him to go back to the beginning of the sentences and recite them again to jog his memory. If necessary, you may then prompt the student with single words.

Watch the student as he writes, and correct him at once if he begins to make a mistake. When he is finished, tell him to underline the action verbs "clutched" and "walked." Ask the student, "Clutched what?" He should answer "nickel." Tell him that "nickel" is the *direct object* of the verb "clutched." What did Jane clutch? She clutched the nickel. The nickel "receives" the action of the verb "clutched." Tell him to write the initials "d.o." over the word "nickel."

Now tell the student that "walked" is also an action verb, but in this sentence it doesn't have a direct object. Jane walked what? Jane didn't walk anything. She just walked. Not every action verb has a direct object.

Day Five (optional): Creative Writing *Student page 131*

Pull out Student page 131. Write the student's name and the date for her as she watches, or ask her to write the name and date independently.

> **Instructor:** Look at the three cats in the illustration and observe their behavior. Can you come up with a fitting name for each of the cats? You can name just one of them, or all three. You can use personality traits or physical traits to choose your names.

WEEK 15

Day One: Narration Exercise *Student pages 133–135*

***Focus:** Identifying the central narrative thread in a passage*

Pull out Student pages 133–134 and 135. Ask the student to write her name and the date on Student page 135.

Allow the student to read the story on Student pages 133–134, either silently or aloud.

Help the student begin to identify the central elements in the narrative by asking the following questions. She should try to answer these questions without looking back at the story, but if she cannot remember an answer after thinking for a few minutes, allow her to reread. Remind her to answer in complete sentences.

Instructor: What did Kerby first do to the beaker of water?
Student: *He put two drops of chemical into the water.*

Instructor: What happened?
Student: *Nothing happened.*

Instructor: What did he decide to do with the beaker?
Student: *He decided to empty it.*

Instructor: What did he do with the water on his way to the bathroom?
Student: *He drank it.*

Instructor: Why did Kerby rush into the bathroom to look at himself in the mirror?
Student: *He was afraid that he would turn into a horrible monster.*

Now ask the student the general question, "Can you give me a brief summary of this passage?" The student should answer by summarizing the plot, rather than listing details. Her answer should be no more than three sentences and should resemble one of the following:

> "Kerby put two drops of chemical into a beaker of water, but nothing happened. He decided to dump the water out. Instead, he sniffed it, and it smelled so good that he drank it."
>
> "Kerby had a mysterious chemistry set. He mixed one of the chemicals into water. Then, without really meaning to, he drank the water."
>
> "Kerby mixed chemicals and water together. Nothing happened, but the water smelled so good that he drank it. Then he was afraid he would change into a horrible monster."

If the student has difficulty condensing the story, ask the following three questions:

What is Kerby's first experiment?

What does he do with the water?

Why is he afraid?

Then have the student repeat her answers in order; this will form her brief summary. Write down the student's narration on Student page 135 as she watches.

When done, set the workbook page aside for the next lesson, which is on the back of it.

Day Two: Dictation Exercise *Student page 136*

Focus: *Semicolons and commas*

Pull out Student page 136. Ask the student to write her name and the date.

Tell the student that today's dictation sentence is from Robert Louis Stevenson's story *Dr. Jekyll and Mr. Hyde.* Dr. Jekyll makes a potion that turns him into an evil man named Mr. Hyde. In this sentence, one of Dr. Jekyll's friends goes to see him.

Dictate the following sentence to the student three times. Before you read, tell the student that you will read the sentence four times before asking her to write, and will not repeat it afterwards. (This is a complicated sentence, so you will add an extra repetition.)

Tell the student that this sentence has the name "Dr. Jekyll" in it, and that "Doctor" should be spelled as the abbreviation "Dr."

Tell the student that this long sentence is actually three shorter sentences, attached to each other by semicolons. There are also commas in the sentence. You will pause for a brief time at each comma and for a longer time at each semicolon.

When you read the sentence, let your voice fall on the words that precede each semicolon, so that the student can hear the end of each short sentence.

> The fire burned in the grate; a lamp was set lighted on the chimney shelf, for even in the houses the fog began to lie thickly; and there, close up to the warmth, sat Dr. Jekyll, looking deadly sick.

Now ask the student to repeat the sentence back to you before she writes. If she forgets, tell her to go back to the beginning of the sentence and recite it again to jog her memory. If necessary, you may then prompt the student with single words.

Watch the student as she writes, and correct her at once if she begins to make a mistake. You will probably need to help her spell the name "Jekyll."

Day Three: Narration and Dictation *Student pages 137–139*

Focus: *Identifying the central theme in a selection and writing original sentences from dictation*

Pull out Student pages 137–138 and 139. Ask the student to write her name and the date on Student page 139.

Allow the student to read the story on Student pages 137–138, either silently or aloud.

Now help the student begin to identify the central theme in the selection by asking the following questions. She should try to answer these questions without looking back at the story, but if she cannot remember an answer after thinking for a few minutes, allow her to reread. Remind her to answer in complete sentences.

Instructor: There are several different meanings of the word "good." Kerby might be feeling "good" because he feels energetic and happy. Or he might be feeling "good" because he feels like doing the right thing. Which meaning of "good" is the correct one for this story?
Student: *He feels like doing the right thing.*

Instructor: What did he do to the beaker?
Student: *He rinsed it and dried it.*

Instructor: For what did Kerby apologize to Waldo?
Student: *He apologized for dragging Waldo down the hall by the tail.*

Instructor: What did he decide to do to the floors?
Student: *He decided to polish them.*

Instructor: Why did he decide not to do any more experiments in his room?
Student: *He might spill the chemicals and mark his furniture.*

Instructor: What did he then go outside and do?
Student: *He mowed the lawn.*

Instructor: He did two extra things when he mowed the lawn. What were they?
Student: *He trimmed around the trees and fence, and he put the grass clippings on the compost heap.*

Instructor: Do you think that Kerby normally did such a good job cutting the lawn?
Student: *No, he probably didn't.*

Instructor: Why did Kerby's mother nearly fall on her face with surprise?
Student: *Kerby had already fixed lunch.*

Instructor: What did Kerby do all afternoon?
Student: *He worked in the basement.*

Instructor: How did his mother react to this?
Student: *She wondered if he was sick OR She kept asking him if he was all right OR She called his father.*

Now say to the student, "Try to tell me, in one sentence, how Kerby felt after drinking the water in the beaker." The student should respond, "Kerby felt like doing good things," or "Kerby felt helpful and good." The answer should reflect the *ethical* character of Kerby's "feeling good." Prompt the student, if she seems uncertain, by asking the first comprehension question again.

Once the student has come up with this sentence, say, "Now give me two more sentences with specific details in them about the good things Kerby did." The purpose of this exercise is to guide the student into stating the central theme of the passage and supporting that theme with specifics.

The answer should resemble one of the following:

> "Kerby felt like doing good things. He apologized to Waldo for dragging him down the hall by the tail. Then he cut the grass, fixed lunch, and cleaned up the basement."
>
> "Kerby felt like doing good things. He put his chemistry set neatly away and decided not to play with it in his room. Then he cut the grass, trimmed around the fence, put the clippings on the compost pile, and fixed lunch."
>
> "Kerby felt helpful and good. He decided to polish the floors for his mother. He cut the grass, cleaned the cellar, and fixed lunch for his mother."

Write down the student's narration on the lines below, but do not allow her to watch.

____

____

____

____

Then choose two or three sentences (15–18 words) to dictate back to the student. Repeat the sentences three times and ask the student to repeat them back to you before she writes on Student page 139.

Give all necessary help in spelling and punctuation.

When done, set the workbook page aside for the next lesson, which is on the back of it.

Day Four: Dictation Exercise — *Student page 140*

***Focus:** Direct objects following action verbs*

Pull out Student page 140. Ask the student to write her name and the date.

Tell the student that today's dictation sentence is also from Robert Louis Stevenson's story *Dr. Jekyll and Mr. Hyde*. In it, Dr. Jekyll describes making and drinking the potion that will change him into the evil Mr. Hyde.

Dictate the following sentence to the student three times. Before you read, tell the student that you will read the sentence only three times before asking her to write, and will not repeat it afterwards.

Tell the student that there are no semicolons in this sentence, just commas.

> Late one accursed night, I compounded the elements, watched them boil and smoke together in the glass, and then, with a strong glow of courage, drank the potion.

Now ask the student to repeat the sentence back to you before she writes. Remind her to pause at the commas. If she forgets, tell her to go back to the beginning of the sentence and recite it again to jog her memory.

If necessary, you may then prompt the student with single words.

Watch the student as she writes, and correct her at once if she begins to make a mistake. When she is finished, tell her to underline the action verbs "compounded," "watched," and "drank." (You may need to explain that "compounded" means "mixed together.") Tell the student that each one of these action verbs has a direct object.

> What is the direct object of "compounded?" (The correct answer is "elements." What did he compound? He compounded the elements.) Tell her to write the initials "d.o." over the direct object "elements."
>
> What is the direct object of "watched?" (The correct answer is "them." What did he watch? He watched them. "Them" is a pronoun, referring back to the elements.) Tell her to write the initials "d.o." over the direct object "them."
>
> What is the direct object of "drank?" (The correct answer is "potion." What did he drink? He drank the potion.) Tell her to write the initials "d.o." over the direct object "potion."

Day Five (optional): Creative Writing *Student page 141*

Pull out Student page 141. Write the student's name and the date for him as he watches, or ask him to write the name and date independently.

> **Instructor:** Imagine you could make a magical lemonade that could change people's behavior. What would your lemonade make them do? If you like, draw a picture of someone who has had a drink of your magic lemonade.

WEEK 16

DAY ONE: Narration Exercise *Student pages 143–145*

***Focus:** Summarizing a series of ordered facts*

Pull out Student pages 143–144 and 145. Ask the student to write his name and the date on Student page 145.

Allow the student to read the selection on Student pages 143–144, either silently or aloud.

Help the student summarize the steps outlined in the passage, in order, by asking the following questions. He should try to answer these questions without looking back at the story, but if he cannot remember an answer after thinking for a few minutes, allow him to reread. Remind him to answer in complete sentences.

Instructor: What is the first step in setting up the trick?
Student: *Make a candleholder of clay and put the candle in it.*

Instructor: What is the second step in setting up the trick?
Student: *Put the coin in the dish and cover it with water.*

Instructor: What is the third step in setting up the trick?
Student: *Put food coloring in the water.*

Instructor: What is the audience challenged to do?
Student: *They are challenged to remove the coin without getting their fingers wet.*

Instructor: What is the first step in solving the problem?
Student: *Put the candle and candleholder in the dish.*

Instructor: What is the second step in solving the problem?
Student: *Light the candle.*

Instructor: What is the third step in solving the problem?
Student: *Put the glass over the lit candle.*

Instructor: What happens to the water after the candle uses up the oxygen and goes out?
Student: *Water is pushed up into the glass.*

Instructor: What happens to the dish?
Student: *The dish is dry.*

Instructor: What does the candle use up when it burns?
Student: *The candle uses oxygen.*

Now say to the student, "First, tell me how to set up the trick. Then, tell me how to solve the problem." His answer should be no more than four sentences and should resemble one of the following:

"Set a candle in a clay candleholder. Put a coin in a dish and cover it with colored water. Then set the candle in the dish and light it. Put a glass over the candle, and the water will be pushed up into the glass."

"Put a coin in a dish and cover it with water. Put a few drops of food coloring in the water. Set a candle in the dish, light it, and put a glass over it. When the candle uses the oxygen, the water will be pushed up into the glass."

"Put enough colored water in a dish to cover a coin. Set a lit candle in the dish, far away from the coin. Put a glass over the coin. When the candle uses the oxygen in the glass, water will be sucked away from the coin up into the glass."

Write down the student's narration on Student page 145 as he watches.

When done, set the workbook page aside for the next lesson, which is on the back of it.

Day Two: Dictation Exercise *Student page 146*

Focus: *Linking verbs and predicate nominatives*

Pull out Student page 146. Ask the student to write his name and the date.

Dictate the following sentences to the student three times. Before you read, tell the student that you will read the sentences only three times before asking him to write, and will not repeat them afterwards.

Tell the student that today's dictation is taken from the book *Oxygen* by Michele Thomas. The dictation is three sentences long, and one of the sentences is a question. Ask the student what punctuation mark ends a question. Tell the student to listen for the end of each sentence.

Also tell the student that there are two commas in the sentences. Ask him to listen for the pauses that indicate commas.

When you read the dictation, be sure to indicate the question with your voice. Indicate the end of the second sentence by allowing your voice to fall. Pause at the commas in the third sentence.

> Can you smell the oxygen in the air? Probably not. Oxygen is an odorless, tasteless, and colorless element.

Now ask the student to repeat the sentences back to you before he writes. If he forgets, tell him to go back to the beginning of the sentences and recite them again to jog his memory.

If necessary, you may then prompt the student with single words.

Watch the student as he writes, and correct him at once if he begins to make a mistake. You may need to spell "oxygen" for him.

When he is finished, ask him to underline the word "oxygen" in the third sentence. This is the subject of the sentence. Now ask him to circle the verb "is." This is a state of being verb. (If he knows the state of being verbs, have him chant them now.) In this sentence, however, the state of being verb becomes a linking verb. It links the subject "oxygen" to the noun "element." What is oxygen? Oxygen is an element.

"Element" is a predicate nominative. It is a noun that *renames* the subject. "Oxygen" and "element" are the same thing.

DAY THREE: Narration and Dictation *Student pages 147–148*

***Focus:** Summarizing a series of ordered facts and writing original sentences from dictation*

Pull out Student pages 147 and 148. Ask the student to write his name and the date on Student page 148.

Allow the student to read the selection on Student page 147, either silently or aloud.

Help the student summarize the steps outlined in the passage, in order, by asking the following questions. He should try to answer these questions without looking back at the story, but if he cannot remember an answer after thinking for a few minutes, allow him to reread. Remind him to answer in complete sentences.

Instructor: What do you tell the audience you can do?
Student: *You tell them you can read minds.*

Instructor: What does the audience do after you go out of the room?
Student: *The audience chooses an object.*

Instructor: When you come back in, what does your volunteer do?
Student: *Your volunteer points to several objects.*

Instructor: When do you say, "I can read your mind. That is the correct object!"
Student: *You say this when the volunteer points to the object chosen by the audience.*

Instructor: What have you and the volunteer decided ahead of time?
Student: *You have decided on a set of signals.*

Instructor: Give me an example of a signal you might use. (Hint: the signal I want uses the color "red.")
Student: *The volunteer points to something red right before he points to the correct object.*

Instructor: What hand should the volunteer point with if the object itself is red?
Student: *He should point with his left hand.*

Instructor: If the correct object is red and the volunteer is using his left hand, what color object should he point to *before* he points to the correct object?
Student: *He should point to a black object.*

Now say to the student, "Tell me in two or three sentences how you and the volunteer set up the trick." His answer should be no more than three sentences and should resemble one of the following:

"You decide that the volunteer will point to a red object right before the correct object. If the correct object is red, he will use his left hand and point to a black object right before."

"You choose your volunteer ahead of time. You decide on signals. Before he points to the right object, he will point to a red object, or he will point to a black object with his left hand."

"You and the volunteer decide on signals ahead of time. Before he points to the right object, he will point to a red object. If the object itself is red, he will point to a black object with his left hand right before he points to the correct object."

Write down the student's narration on the lines below, but do not allow him to watch.

____

____

____

____

Then choose two or three sentences (15–18 words) to dictate back to the student. Repeat the sentences three times and ask the student to repeat them back to you before he writes on Student page 148.

Give all necessary help in spelling and punctuation.

Day Four: Dictation Exercise *Student page 149*

Focus: *Linking verbs and predicate adjectives*

Pull out Student page 149. Ask the student to write his name and the date.

Tell the student that today's dictation sentence is from *101 Easy-to-Do Magic Tricks* by Bill Tarr. The sentence is about "presentation"—the art of doing a magic trick in a way that entertains the audience.

Dictate the following sentence to the student three times. Before you read, tell the student that you will read the sentence only three times before asking him to write, and will not repeat it afterwards.

Tell the student to listen carefully for the commas in the sentence, and then pause significantly at each one. Do not tell him ahead of time how many commas there are.

> Good presentation is clear, direct, easy to follow, and as interesting and absorbing as you can make it.

Now ask the student to repeat the sentence back to you before he writes. If he forgets, tell him to go back to the beginning of the sentence and recite it again to jog his memory. If necessary, you may then prompt the student with single words.

Watch the student as he writes, and correct him at once if he begins to make a mistake.

When he is finished, ask him to underline the word "presentation" in the sentence. This is the subject of the sentence. Now ask him to circle the verb "is." This is a state of being verb. (If he knows the state of being verbs, have him chant them now.) In this sentence, however, the state of being verb becomes a linking verb. It links the subject "presentation" to several adjectives that describe *what* good presentation is.

Say to the student, "What is good presentation? Underline each word that tells you what good presentation is." The student should underline "clear," "direct," "easy," "interesting," and "absorbing." These are all adjectives that describe "presentation." (If the student asks, tell him that "to follow" is a verb that tells more about "easy," not more about "presentation.")

Now tell the student that because those adjectives come after the linking verb, they are called *predicate adjectives.* Have the student draw an arrow from each predicate adjective back to the subject.

When done, set the workbook page aside for the next lesson, which is on the back of it.

Day Five (optional): Creative Writing *Student page 150*

Pull out Student page 150. Write the student's name and the date for her as she watches, or ask her to write the name and date independently.

> **Instructor:** If you were a magician, what trick would you to amaze your audience? You don't have to explain how the trick works – just describe what the audience would see.

WEEK 17

Day One: Narration Exercise *Student pages 151–153*

Focus: *Summarizing a series of ordered facts*

Pull out Student pages 151–152 and 153. Ask the student to write her name and the date on Student page 153.

Allow the student to read the selection on Student pages 151–152, either silently or aloud.

Help the student summarize the steps outlined in the passage, in order, by asking the following questions. She should try to answer these questions without looking back at the story, but if she cannot remember an answer after thinking for a few minutes, allow her to reread. Remind her to answer in complete sentences.

Instructor: The magician tells Ehrich that what a magician actually *does* doesn't really count. What counts?
Student: *What people think you do counts.*

Instructor: When the magician shows the empty bucket with his left hand, what else is he holding in his left hand?
Student: *He is holding coins in his left hand.*

Instructor: Why doesn't the audience see the coins?
Student: *They are looking at the empty bucket.*

Instructor: What does he have in his right hand?
Student: *He has one coin.*

Instructor: Describe how the magician holds the coin in his right hand so that no one can see it. [Note: if the student has trouble answering, you may want to give her a coin to hold between her thumb and first finger so that the coin cannot be seen from the front of her hand.]
Student: *He holds the coin between his thumb and first finger.*

Instructor: When the magician picks a coin out of the air, what is he really doing?
Student: *He is showing the audience the coin already in his hand.*

Instructor: What does he do next with that coin?
Student: *He slips it to the back of his hand again.*

Instructor: Where does he get the coin that goes in the bucket?
Student: *He gets it from his left hand.*

Now say to the student, "Describe how the magician did the coin trick." Her answer should be no more than three sentences and should resemble one of the following:

"The magician hid coins in his left hand and one coin in his right hand. He showed the coin in his right hand and pretended to pick it out of the air. Then he hid that coin again and put a coin into the bucket from his left hand."

"The magician held a bucket and hidden coins with his left hand. He held one coin in his right hand. He pretended to pick the coin in his right hand out of the air and dropped coins from his left hand into the bucket."

"The magician hid a coin in his right hand. He showed the coin and pretended to pick it out of the air, and then hid the coin and pretended to put it in the bucket. Meanwhile, he put coins from his left hand into the bucket."

Write down the student's narration on Student page 153 as she watches.

When done, set the workbook page aside for the next lesson, which is on the back of it.

Day Two: Dictation Exercise *Student page 154*

Focus: *Linking verbs and predicate nominatives*

Pull out Student page 154. Tell the student that today's dictation sentence is from a book called *The Right Way to Do Wrong* by Harry Houdini himself. Houdini spent many years studying the tricks that criminals use. Here's what Houdini writes in the first chapter of his book: "The object of this book is . . . to safeguard the public against the practices of the criminal classes by exposing their various tricks and explaining the adroit methods by which they seek to defraud. 'Knowledge is power' is an old saying. I might paraphrase it in this case by saying knowledge is safety. I wish to put the public on its guard, so that honest folks may be able to detect and protect themselves from the dishonest, who labor under the false impression that it is easier to live dishonestly than to thrive by honest means."

Dictate the following sentences to the student three times. Before you read, tell the student that you will read the sentences only three times before asking her to write, and will not repeat them afterwards.

> "Knowledge is power" is an old saying. I might paraphrase it by saying knowledge is safety.

Now ask the student to repeat the sentences back to you before she writes. If she forgets, tell her to go back to the beginning of the sentences and recite them again to jog her memory. If necessary, you may then prompt the student with single words.

Before she begins to write, tell her that the phrase "Knowledge is power" has quotation marks around it. The quotation marks show that Houdini is not using his own words—he is using the words of a traditional saying. (If the student asks, you may also tell her that there is no comma after "power," as there would be in dialogue, because this is not something that Houdini himself is saying out loud.) The phrase "knowledge is safety" doesn't have quotation marks because Houdini is now using his own words.

Watch the student as she writes, and correct her at once if she begins to make a mistake.

When she is finished, point out that there are two predicate nominatives in these sentences. Both of them rename "knowledge." Ask the student to find and circle them. (The correct answers are "power" and "safety.") Both predicate nominatives are linked to "knowledge" by the linking verb "is."

Day Three: Narration and Dictation *Student pages 155–157*

Focus: *Summarizing a series of ordered facts and writing original sentences from dictation*

Pull out Student pages 151–156 and 157. Ask the student to write her name and the date on Student page 157.

Allow the student to read the selection on Student pages 155–156, either silently or aloud.

Help the student summarize the steps outlined in the passage, in order, by asking the following questions. She should try to answer these questions without looking back at the story, but if she cannot remember an answer after thinking for a few minutes, allow her to reread. Remind her to answer in complete sentences.

Instructor: During the magic trick itself, what was Houdini wearing when he got into the box?
Student: *He was wearing handcuffs and chains.*

Instructor: What did carpenters do to the box?
Student: *They nailed the top shut.*

Instructor: What was placed in front of the box?
Student: *A drapery cabinet stood in front of the box.*

Instructor: When Houdini appeared, what did the box look like?
Student: *It was still nailed closed.*

Instructor: How did Houdini and his assistant actually prepare the box?
Student: *They replaced the nails on one side with short nails.*

Instructor: What did Houdini do as soon as he got out of the box?
Student: *He tapped the long nails back in.*

Instructor: Why didn't the audience hear him?
Student: *The band was playing loudly.*

Instructor: What tool did Houdini use at other times to get out of the box?
Student: *He used a steel jack hidden in his clothes.*

Instructor: Why didn't the audience hear him?
Student: *The band was playing loudly.*

Instructor: Can you remember three of the strange things Houdini escaped from on his American tour?
Student: *He escaped from an envelope, a glass box, a coffin, a sausage skin, and a giant football.*

Now say to the student, "Tell the two ways that Houdini escaped from his boxes." Her answer should be no more than three sentences and should resemble one of the following:

> "Houdini and his assistant replaced the long nails in the box with short nails. When no one could see, Houdini pushed the small nails out and nailed the long ones back in. Sometimes Houdini smuggled a steel jack into the box and used that instead."
>
> "Houdini's assistant prepared the box ahead of time by using short nails that were easy to push out. After Houdini pushed the box apart he nailed it back together while the band played. Houdini also used a small steel jack hidden in his clothes to push the box apart."
>
> "Houdini could push the box apart because some of the nails had been taken out and replaced with small ones. Sometimes he also pried the box apart with a hidden steel jack. Afterwards he nailed the box back together while the band played loudly."

Write down the student's narration on the lines below, but do not allow her to watch.

____

____

____

____

Then choose two or three sentences (15–18 words) to dictate back to the student. Repeat the sentences three times and ask the student to repeat them back to you before she writes on Student page 157.

Give all necessary help in spelling and punctuation.

When done, set the workbook page aside for the next lesson, which is on the back of it.

DAY FOUR: Dictation Exercise *Student page 158*

Focus: *Linking verbs, predicate nominatives, and predicate adjectives*

Pull out Student page 158. Ask the student to write her name and the date.

Tell the student that today's dictation sentences are also from Harry Houdini's book about criminals, *The Right Way to Do Wrong*. In this paragraph, Houdini describes pickpockets:

"Among the most interesting classes of thieves is the pickpocket, whose clever subterfuges and skill of hand have been so often exploited in novel and story-book . . . It is the usual opinion that a pickpocket is a forbidding and suspicious looking fellow, but a glance at the rogues' gallery in any police headquarters will show you that they look much like ordinary individuals, and are of more than average intelligence."

Dictate the following sentences to the student three times. Before you read, tell the student that you will read the sentences only three times before asking her to write, and will not repeat them afterwards.

You will probably need to tell the student that "prepossessing" means "attractive, creating a good impression."

> The pickpocket is usually very well dressed and of prepossessing appearance. They are entertaining talkers and easy in their manner.

Now ask the student to repeat the sentence back to you before she writes. If she forgets, tell her to go back to the beginning of the sentences and recite them again to jog her memory. If necessary, you may then prompt the student with single words.

Watch the student as she writes, and correct her at once if she begins to make a mistake. You may need to help her spell "prepossessing." When she is finished, point out that there is a predicate adjective in the second sentence. It describes "they." Ask the student to find and circle it. (The correct answer is "easy.") There is also a predicate nominative, which renames "they" (it is "talkers"). Both of these are linked to the subject "they" by the linking verb "are."

DAY FIVE (optional): Creative Writing *Student page 159*

Pull out Student page 159. Write the student's name and the date for him as he watches, or ask him to write the name and date independently.

Instructor: Complete the story below by adding 1-2 sentences:

I ran to the bathroom and looked in the mirror. Nobody stood in the reflection. "The potion worked," I exclaimed. "I'm invisible!" I knew just what to do next . . .

If you like, draw an illustration to go with your story.

WEEK 18

Day One: Narration Exercise *Student pages 161–163*

***Focus:** Identifying the central theme in a selection*

Pull out Student pages 161–162 and 163. Ask the student to write his name and the date on Student page 163.

Allow the student to read the story on Student pages 161–162 either silently or aloud.

Help the student begin to identify the central theme in the selection by asking the following questions. He should try to answer these questions without looking back at the story, but if he cannot remember an answer after thinking for a few minutes, allow him to reread. Remind him to answer in complete sentences.

Instructor: How many cooks at a time could work in Paul Bunyan's new kitchen?
Student: *Two hundred cooks at a time could work in the kitchen.*

Instructor: How long were the tables in the dining room?
Student: *The tables were six miles long.*

Instructor: How many gallons of soup could the kettle hold?
Student: *It could hold eleven hundred gallons.*

Instructor: How did Hot Biscuit Slim get vegetables into the soup?
Student: *He rowed into the kettle with boatloads of vegetables and shoveled them in.*

Instructor: How did the cookhouse boys grease the ten-acre griddle?
Student: *They strapped bacon onto their feet and skated back and forth.*

Instructor: How many men did one hot cake feed?
Student: *It fed five men.*

Instructor: What did Slim say that hurt Cream Puff Fatty's pride?
Student: *He said that the men wouldn't be able to eat dessert.*

Instructor: What did Cream Puff Fatty decide to cook for dessert?
Student: *He made cream puffs with whipped cream a foot high.*

Instructor: Name three things that Hot Biscuit Slim served for Sunday dinner.
Student: *He served soup, vegetables, salads, chicken pie, hot biscuits with jelly, spinach, cucumbers, and young red radishes.*

Instructor: Did the men eat the cream puffs anyway?
Student: *Yes, they did.*

Now say to the student, "Try to complete this sentence with one interesting, vivid word. 'Everything in Paul Bunyan's camp was. . . .'" The student will probably say "big." Help him find another, more vivid word. If necessary, you can offer him the following list to look at:

colossal

enormous

gigantic

huge

immense

mammoth

oversize

tremendous

vast

Once the student has come up with this sentence, say, "Give me two more sentences with two or more details about the size of Paul Bunyan's camp." The purpose of this exercise is to guide the student into stating the central theme of the passage and supporting that theme with specifics.

The answer should resemble one of the following:

> "Paul Bunyan's camp was enormous. The dining tables were six miles long, and the soup kettle was so huge that the cook had to row into the middle of it with his boat filled with vegetables. The cookboys greased the griddle by skating on it, and the hot cakes were so big that it took five men to eat one."

> "Paul Bunyan's camp was gigantic. Two hundred cooks worked on the meals. The meals were so huge that the men ate soup, vegetables, salads, chicken pie, hot biscuits with jelly, and cream puffs a foot tall."

> "Paul Bunyan's camp was oversize. The kettle held eleven hundred gallons, the griddle was ten acres across, and the dining tables were six miles long. The men were served so much food that it took two hundred cooks to prepare it, and boys on roller skates served it."

Write down the student's narration on Student page 163.

When done, set the workbook page aside for the next lesson, which is on the back of it.

Day Two: Dictation Exercise *Student page 164*

***Focus:** Linking verbs, predicate nominatives and predicate adjectives*

Pull out Student page 164. Ask the student to write his name and the date.

Dictate the following sentence to the student three times. Before you read, tell the student that you will read the sentence only three times before asking him to write, and will not repeat it afterwards.

Pause at the comma, but do not tell the student that the comma is there.

> **By the time Paul Bunyan was sixteen years old, he was the best logger in his father's camp in the Maine woods.**

Now ask the student to repeat the sentence back to you before he writes. If he forgets, tell him to go back to the beginning of the sentence and recite it again to jog his memory. If necessary, you may then prompt the student with single words.

Watch the student as he writes, and correct him at once if he begins to make a mistake. You may need to remind him that "father's" has an apostrophe to show possession.

When he is finished, tell him to circle both occurrences of the linking verb "was." In the first phrase, "was" links Paul Bunyan to what phrase? "Sixteen years old." The phrase acts as a predicate adjective; it describes Paul Bunyan.

Now tell the student to underline the pronoun "he." In the second part of the sentence, "he" is the subject. Ask the student to underline the noun that renames "he" and to label it "p.n." for "predicate nominative." (The answer is "logger.") Have the student draw an arrow from the word "logger" back to the pronoun "he."

Day Three: Narration and Dictation *Student pages 165–166*

***Focus:** Identifying the central details in a passage and writing original sentences from dictation*

Pull out Student pages 165 and 166. Ask the student to write his name and the date on Student page 166.

Today's exercise will combine narration and dictation. Allow the student to read the selection on Student page 165, either silently or aloud.

Help the student begin to identify the central details in the narrative by asking the following questions. He should try to answer these questions without looking back at the story, but if he cannot remember an answer after thinking for a few minutes, allow him to reread. Remind him to answer in complete sentences.

Instructor: The passage says that families and single young men who came to British Canada took on different tasks. What is one thing families did?
Student: *They cleared the forests OR planted new farms OR built up cities and towns.*

Instructor: What are two things that young men did?
Student: *They dug canals around the rapids and waterfalls, hauled timber, salted down codfish, and worked in shipyards.*

Instructor: From what nation did most of the immigrants come?
Student: *Most of them came from Britain. [If the student answers Scotland, Ireland, or England, tell them that this is correct, but that those countries were part of a larger nation: Britain, or Great Britain.]*

Instructor: What does it mean if a country is "a good poor man's country"?
Student: *Anyone willing to work hard can do well.*

Instructor: What time of year did lumberjacks cut wood?
Student: *They cut wood in the winter.*

Instructor: In the spring, what did they do with the logs?
Student: *They floated the logs down the rapids to the sawmills and timber ships.*

Instructor: People told all sorts of tall tales about the lumberjack Joseph Montferrand. Can you remember three of the things that Montferrand could supposedly do?
Student: *He was so strong no boxer could beat him; he could leave bootmarks on a ceiling and land on his feet; he could drink a lake dry; he could dig a channel by dragging his axe; he combed his hair with a pine tree.*

Now ask the student the general question, "Can you give me a brief summary of this passage? Be sure to tell me where the immigrants came from and what at least two groups of them did." His answer should be around three sentences long (he may add a sentence about Joseph Monteferrand for a four-sentence option) and should resemble one of the following:

> "Families and young men came from Britain to look for work. Many of the families cleared forests, planted farms, and built towns. Young men became lumberjacks, fishermen or shipbuilders."
>
> "Immigrants came from England, Scotland, and Ireland to British Canada. Families built new farms and cities, while young men cut wood, dug canals, and fished. Lumberjacks cut timber all winter long and then rode the logs down the rivers in the spring."
>
> "British immigrants came to Canada to find new lives and new work. Families cleared forests and built cities and towns. Many young men became lumberjacks, a job which only the strongest men could do. One famous lumberjack was so strong that people said he could drink a lake dry and comb his hair with a pine tree."

Write down the student's narration on the lines below, but do not allow him to watch.

Then choose two or three sentences (15–18 words) to dictate back to the student. Repeat the sentences three times and ask the student to repeat them back to you before he writes on Student page 166.

Give all necessary help in spelling and punctuation.

DAY FOUR: Dictation Exercise *Student page 167*

***Focus:** Linking verbs and predicate nominatives*

Pull out Student page 167. Ask the student to write his name and the date.

Dictate the following sentence to the student three times. Before you read, tell the student that you will read the sentence only three times before asking him to write, and will not repeat it afterwards.

Pause significantly at the comma, but do not tell the student ahead of time that the comma is there.

> All through the nineteenth century, lumbering was the greatest industry in many parts of eastern Canada.

Now ask the student to repeat the sentence back to you before he writes. If he forgets, tell him to go back to the beginning of the sentence and recite it again to jog his memory. If necessary, you may then prompt the student with single words.

Watch the student as he writes, and correct him at once if he begins to make a mistake. When he finishes, point out that there is a predicate nominative in the second half of the sentence. It is a noun that describes "lumbering." Ask him to find and circle it. (The correct answer is "industry.") It is linked to the subject, "lumbering," by the linking verb "was."

When done, set the workbook page aside for the next lesson, which is on the back of it.

DAY FIVE (optional): Creative Writing *Student page 168*

Pull out Student page 168. Write the student's name and the date for her as she watches, or ask her to write the name and date independently.

> **Instructor:** Imagine that you transformed into a giant for one day. What would you do that day? If you like, draw yourself as a giant.

WEEK 19

Day One: Narration Exercise *Student pages 169–171*

***Focus:** Identifying the central narrative thread in a passage*

Pull out Student pages 169–170 and 171. Ask the student to write her name and the date on Student page 171.

Allow the student to read the story on Student pages 169–170, either silently or aloud.

Help the student begin to identify the central elements in the narrative by asking the following questions. She should try to answer these questions without looking back at the story, but if she cannot remember an answer after thinking for a few minutes, allow her to reread. Remind her to answer in complete sentences.

Instructor: What kind of rule did the Americans believe to be wrong?
Student: *They believed that absolute rule was wrong.*

Instructor: What had Americans been doing for the last one hundred and fifty years?
Student: *They had been making their own laws.*

Instructor: What did the members of the Continental Congress decide to declare about the colonies?
Student: *They decided to declare the American colonies independent.*

Instructor: Who was chosen to write the official declaration?
Student: *Thomas Jefferson was chosen.*

Instructor: How long did Jefferson work on writing the declaration?
Student: *He worked for two weeks.*

Instructor: The first part of the Declaration of Independence explains American beliefs about what form of government?
Student: *It explains American beliefs about democracy.*

Instructor: Can you remember the three rights that men are born with, according to the Declaration?
Student: *They are born with the right to life, the right to liberty, and the right to try to be happy.*

Instructor: What is a government supposed to do about these rights?
Student: *It is supposed to preserve these rights for all.*

Instructor: The second part of the Declaration contains a list. What does the list describe?
Student: *It describes the tyranny of the king.*

Instructor: How long did the members of the Congress debate the Declaration?
Student: *They debated for almost three days.*

Instructor: When did they approve it?
Student: *They approved it on July 4, 1776.*

Now ask the student the general question, "Can you give me a brief summary of this passage?" The student should answer by summarizing the plot, rather than listing details. She may have four full sentences to answer; her answer should resemble one of the following:

> "Kings had absolute rule, but Americans wanted to make laws for themselves. The Continental Congress decided to declare the American colonies to be independent. Thomas Jefferson was chosen to write the Declaration of Independence. The first part explained that men had certain rights; the second part listed all the ways that the king had refused to honor those rights."
>
> "Americans had been making their own laws for 150 years. The Continental Congress decided to declare America independent of the English king. Thomas Jefferson wrote out the official Declaration of Independence. The Continental Congress approved the Declaration on July 4, 1776."
>
> "The Continental Congress declared the American colonies independent and chose Thomas Jefferson to write the official Declaration. The Declaration said that all men had the right to life, the right to liberty, and the right to try to be happy. It also listed many examples of the king's tyranny."

The student will probably attempt to put too much information into the summary. If she has difficulty condensing the story, ask the following three questions:

> What did Americans believe?
>
> What did the Continental Congress decide to do?
>
> What official document explained this?
>
> What were the two parts of this document, and what did each say?

Then have the student repeat her answers in order; this will form her brief summary.
Write down the student's narration on Student page 171 as she watches.
When done, set the workbook page aside for the next lesson, which is on the back of it.

DAY TWO: Dictation Exercise *Student page 172*

Focus: *Command sentences and understood "you"*

Pull out Student page 172. Ask the student to write her name and the date.

Tell the student that today's dictation sentence is from a letter written by Thomas Jefferson, who also wrote out the Declaration of Independence for the Continental Congress. Tell her that Thomas Jefferson often wrote letters to the members of his family, giving them advice and telling them about his own work. He wrote many of these letters to his young nephew Peter Carr. Jefferson wanted Peter to be as well educated, healthy, and happy as possible. He gave Peter many commands: he told Peter to read many books and to make a special study of ancient history, to go for walks every day, to avoid ever doing a dishonorable thing, to learn French, and to practice shooting a gun.

These sentences are taken from a letter that Jefferson wrote to Peter Carr in 1785, when Peter was fifteen years old.

Dictate the following sentences to the student three times. Before you read, tell the student that you will read the sentences only three times before asking her to write, and will not repeat them afterwards.

Pause significantly at the comma, and for an even longer time at the period; also indicate the end of the first sentence by allowing your voice to fall. However, do not tell the student ahead of time about the comma or period.

> Write to me once every month or two, and let me know the progress you make. Tell me in what manner you employ every hour in the day.

Now ask the student to repeat the sentences back to you before she writes. If she forgets, tell her to go back to the beginning of the sentences and recite them again to jog her memory. If necessary, you may then prompt the student with single words.

Watch the student as she writes, and correct her at once if she begins to make a mistake. When she is finished, tell her to underline the words "write," "let," and "tell." Explain that each one is the verb of a command sentence. Jefferson is ordering his nephew to write, to let, and to tell.

Tell the student that, in a command sentence, the subject is understood. Jefferson's nephew is not actually *in* the sentences, but he is the one who is supposed to write, let, and tell.

If Thomas Jefferson were standing right next to young Peter Carr, he might turn around and point at Peter and say, "You write to me! You let me know! You tell me!" In a command sentence, the subject is "understood you." The "you" is not written, but we understand without being told that it is there.

Day Three: Narration and Dictation *Student pages 173–175*

***Focus:** Identifying the central narrative thread in a passage and writing original sentences from dictation*

Pull out Student pages 173–174 and 175. Ask the student to write her name and the date on Student page 175.

Today's exercise will combine narration and dictation. Allow the student to read the story on Student pages 173–174, either silently or aloud.

Help the student begin to identify the central elements in the narrative by asking the following questions. She should try to answer these questions without looking back at the story, but if she cannot remember an answer after thinking for a few minutes, allow her to reread. Remind her to answer in complete sentences.

Instructor: What was the first bad thing John did (or was suspected of doing) that made him unpopular?
Student: *He may have murdered his nephew Arthur of Brittany.*

Instructor: What happened to John's lands in France?
Student: *He lost them.*

Instructor: What nickname did he get for this?
Student: *He became known as "Softsword."*

Instructor: How did John raise money to attack the French and get his lands back?
Student: *He raised taxes.*

Instructor: Even with all this money, was his army able to defeat the French?
Student: *No, his army was defeated.*

Instructor: What did the English people and their leaders force John to sign?
Student: *They forced him to sign the Magna Carta.*

Instructor: According to the passage, what two things did John promise in the Magna Carta?
Student: *He promised to treat everyone more fairly, and he agreed that people could complain to a committee of twenty-five barons if he did not keep his promises.*

Instructor: Did he keep his promises?
Student: *No, he did not.*

Instructor: What did the barons do to get rid of John?
Student: *They chose Louis of France to be the new king of England.*

Instructor: Who actually became king after John died?
Student: *John's son Henry became king.*

Instructor: Was Henry supposed to follow the Magna Carta?
Student: *Yes, he was.*

Now ask the student the general question, "Can you give me a brief summary of this passage?" The student should answer by summarizing the plot, rather than listing details. Her answer should be no more than four sentences and should resemble one of the following:

> "King John of England got rid of his nephew and taxed his people heavily. His people and their leaders forced him to sign the Magna Carta. This said that he would treat people more fairly, and that his people could complain to the barons. John did not keep his promises, but when his son became king, the Magna Carta was reissued."

> "King John became unpopular because he raised taxes and lost land to the French. The English people rebelled. They forced John to agree that he would treat them more fairly.

> The treaty they forced him to sign was called the Magna Carta, but John did not keep the promises he made in it."
>
> "King John became so unpopular that his people forced him to sign the Magna Carta. This treaty said that he would treat everyone more fairly, and that his people could complain to a committee of barons. When John didn't keep his promises, the barons made a French prince king of England instead. Finally John's son became king after John's death."

If she has difficulty condensing the story, ask the following four questions:

> Why was King John unpopular?
>
> What did his people force him to do?
>
> What two things did the Magna Carta say?
>
> Did John keep his promises?

Then have the student repeat her answers in order; this will form her brief summary. Write down the student's narration on the lines below, but do not allow her to watch.

____

____

____

____

Then choose two or three sentences (15–18 words) to dictate back to the student. Repeat the sentences three times and ask the student to repeat them back to you before she writes on Student page 175.

Give all necessary help in spelling and punctuation.

When done, set the workbook page aside for the next lesson, which is on the back of it.

Day Four: Dictation Exercise *Student page 176*

Focus: *Command sentences*

Pull out Student page 176. Ask the student to write her name and the date.

Tell the student that today's dictation sentences are adapted from the Magna Carta. The Magna Carta promised the people of England that no man could be thrown in jail or punished unless it could be proved that he had broken the law. The king of England could no longer arrest men just because he wanted to show his power. This is a paraphrase of the clause that guarantees this freedom (Clause 29). Today we call this right *habeas corpus.*

Dictate the following sentence to the student three times. Before you read, tell the student that you will read the sentence only three times before asking her to write, and will not repeat it afterwards.

Pause significantly at each comma, but do not tell the student that the commas are there.

> No free man shall be imprisoned, or be deprived of his land or liberty, or be exiled or outlawed, except by the law of the land.

Now ask the student to repeat the sentence back to you before she writes. If she forgets, tell her to go back to the beginning of the sentence and recite it again to jog her memory. If necessary, you may then prompt the student with single words.

Watch the student as she writes, and correct her at once if she begins to make a mistake.

When she is finished, ask her whether this is a command sentence or a simple statement. (The correct answer is "statement"—although the statement has the sound of a command, it is simply announcing a fact.) Point out that the subject of the sentence is "man," rather than "you."

Day Five (optional): Creative Writing *Student page 177*

Pull out Student page 177. Write the student's name and the date for him as he watches, or ask him to write the name and date independently.

Instructor: If you could make a law (or rule) that everyone in the whole world had to follow, what would it be? Write your sentence as a command. If you like, draw a picture of someone breaking your rule and then draw a big red X across your finished illustration to show that this is not allowed.

Note To Instructor: If your student needs help getting started, try providing one of the sentence stems: "No one is allowed to . . ." OR "Everyone must . . ."

WEEK 20

DAY ONE: Narration Exercise *Student pages 179–181*

***Focus:** Identifying the central details in a passage*

Pull out Student pages 179–180 and 181. Ask the student to write his name and the date on Student page 181.

Allow the student to read the story on Student pages 179–180, either silently or aloud.

You will now ask the student to summarize the passage. A detail-oriented summary is more appropriate to this descriptive passage than a summary telling what happens. Since this is the first time the student has summarized without having the help of comprehension questions, use a "directed narration starter." Say to the student, "Describe the garden in three sentences." His answer should resemble one of the following:

> "In the garden, all the flowers can talk. The Tiger-lily is the leader of the flowers. The tree at the center of the garden keeps them safe by saying 'Bough-wow.'"
>
> "The flowers in the garden can all talk. Alice finds out that this is because the ground is so hard that they stay awake. In most gardens, the ground is so soft that the flowers fall asleep."
>
> "The Tiger-lily and the Rose both talk to Alice. The daisies talk too, but they all talk at once and make too much noise. The tree at the center of the garden keeps the flowers safe by 'barking.'"
>
> "The garden has tiger-lilies, roses, and pink daisies in it. All of them can talk because the ground is so hard that it keeps them awake. In the middle of the garden, there is a tree that keeps the flowers safe."

If the student has trouble choosing important details, ask these three questions:

> What flowers are in the garden?
>
> What reason does the Tiger-lily give for the flowers' ability to talk?
>
> What is at the center of the garden?

The answers to these questions will make up the student's summary.

Write the narration down on Student page 181 as the student watches.

When done, set the workbook page aside for the next lesson, which is on the back of it.

Day Two: Dictation Exercise *Student page 182*

Focus: *Direct quotations*

Pull out Student page 182. Ask the student to write his name and the date.

Tell the student that today's dictation sentence is from the same chapter of *Through the Looking-Glass*. In the garden, Alice meets the Red Queen from her chess set, now grown to life size. The Red Queen is quite bossy.

Before reading the selection, remind the student of the proper form for direct quotations. The Red Queen's actual words should be surrounded by quotation marks. The ending punctuation for each of the Red Queen's sentences should go *inside* the closing quotation marks. The phrase "said the Red Queen" is part of the previous sentence, so "said" should not be capitalized. "And" is capitalized because it begins a new sentence. Also remind the student that "Red Queen" is used as a proper name, so both words should be capitalized.

Now tell the student that you will read the selection three times. Be sure to indicate questions and statements with your voice; also, use a different voice for the Red Queen's actual words and your normal voice for the phrase "said the Red Queen."

Tell the student that you will only read the sentences three times and will not repeat them afterwards.

> "Where do you come from?" said the Red Queen. "And where are you going? Look up, speak nicely, and don't twiddle your fingers all the time."

Now ask the student to repeat the sentences back to you before he writes. If he forgets, tell him to go back to the beginning of the sentences and recite them again to jog his memory. If necessary, you may then prompt the student with single words.

Watch the student as he writes, and correct him at once if he begins to make a mistake.

Day Three: Narration and Dictation *Student pages 183–185*

Focus: *Identifying the central narrative thread in a passage and writing original sentences from dictation*

Pull out Student pages 183–184 and 185. Ask the student to write his name and the date on Student page 185.

Today's exercise will combine narration and dictation. Allow the student to read the story on Student pages 183–184, either silently or aloud.

You will now ask the student to summarize the passage. This selection lends itself to a narrative, story-like retelling. To guide the student towards this type of summary, ask him, "In three sentences, what happened at the dinner party?" His answer should resemble one of the following:

> "The Red Queen introduced Alice to the leg of mutton, so then the waiters carried it off. Then she introduced Alice to the plum pudding, but Alice cut a slice out of it anyway. When she did, the pudding spoke to her."
>
> "At the dinner, the Red Queen kept introducing Alice to the food. Then the waiters carried it off, because it isn't polite to eat food that you've been introduced to. Finally Alice cut the pudding—but the pudding talked back to her."
>
> "Alice was hungry, but she couldn't eat her meat because she had been introduced to it. The Red Queen also introduced her to the pudding, but she decided to eat it anyway. When she cut a slice, it said, 'How would like me to cut a slice out of you?'"

If the student has difficulty with this summary, ask the following three questions to help focus his thoughts:

> Why couldn't Alice eat her leg of mutton?
>
> What did she do to the pudding?
>
> What did the pudding do in response?

Then have the student repeat his answers in order; this will form his brief summary. Write down the student's narration on the lines below, but do not allow him to watch.

____

____

____

____

Then choose two or three sentences (16–20 words) to dictate back to the student. Repeat the sentences three times and ask the student to repeat them back to you before he writes on Student page 185.

Give all necessary help in spelling and punctuation.

When done, set the workbook page aside for the next lesson, which is on the back of it.

Day Four: Dictation Exercise — *Student page 186*

Focus: *Comma use*

Pull out Student page 186. Ask the student to write his name and the date.

Tell the student that today's dictation sentences are from the chapter of *Through the Looking-Glass* where Alice meets the two strange brothers, Tweedledum and Tweedledee. Spell those names for the student. Then warn him that this selection is one very long sentence with seven commas in it. Make sure to indicate the commas by pausing significantly when you reach each one.

Dictate the following sentence to the student three times. Before you read, tell the student that you will read the sentence only three times before asking him to write. However, tell the student that you will repeat additional times if necessary, since this is a difficult selection.

> So she wandered on, talking to herself as she went, till, on turning a sharp corner, she came upon two fat little men, so suddenly that she could not help starting back, but in another moment she recovered herself, feeling sure that they must be Tweedledum and Tweedledee.

Now ask the student to repeat the sentence back to you before he writes. If he forgets, tell him to go back to the beginning of the sentence and recite it again to jog his memory. You may repeat the sentence as many additional times as necessary.

Watch the student as he writes, and correct him at once if he begins to make a mistake.

Day Five (optional): Creative Writing *Student page 187*

Pull out Student page 187. Write the student's name and the date for her as she watches, or ask her to write the name and date independently.

From this point onward, student responses to the prompt should be 16-20 words (two longer or three shorter sentences). Repeat the sentences back to your student one at a time. Repeat each sentence up to three times before your student writes it down.

> **Instructor:** Imagine if the food on your dinner plate started talking to you. What would it say? Write a short conversation between you and your dinner using direct quotations. If you like, draw a picture of your talking food.

WEEK 21

DAY ONE: Poetry Exercise *Student page 189*

***Focus:** Definitions of poetic terms*

Pull out Student page 189. Ask the student to write his name and the date.

Allow the student to read the poem on Student page 189, either silently or aloud.

Tell the student that, instead of asking questions about the poem, you are going to discuss it with her.

Remind the student that a "rhyme scheme" is a pattern of rhyming words. Ask the student to fill in the rhyme scheme as in Week 5. If necessary, remind her to give each ending rhyme a letter and write these letters in the blanks at the end of the lines.

The pattern is:

A

A

B

A

B

B

C

B

C

C

D

C

D

D

D

D

(***Optional:*** if the student is interested, you may point out to her that the rhyme scheme of the poem can be divided into quatrains—sets of four lines. Each of the first three quatrains has the same pattern, while the last quatrain has the same rhyme for all four lines.

AABA

BBCB

CCDC

DDDD)

Now ask the student to read the two lines written below the poem out loud, stressing each bolded syllable. Remind her that this is iambic meter, because it falls into this pattern: unstress **stress.**

Ask the student to write "iambic" on the blank that follows "meter (unstress **stress**)." Help her to spell the word properly if necessary.

When done, set the workbook page aside for the next lesson, which is on the back of it.

Day Two: Dictation Exercise *Student page 190*

Focus: *Poetic form, exclamations*

Pull out Student page 190. Ask the student to write her name and the date.

Tell the student that today's dictation sentence is from Robert Frost's poem "Blueberries." Explain that when Robert Frost wrote a poem, he often drew very clear pictures of a natural scene as part of his work. Tell her that you will read her the first lines of "Blueberries." As you read, she should pay attention to how many different words Robert Frost used to describe the blueberries.

> You ought to have seen what I saw on my way
> To the village, through Mortenson's pasture to-day:
> Blueberries as big as the end of your thumb,
> Real sky-blue, and heavy, and ready to drum
> In the cavernous pail of the first one to come!
> And all ripe together, not some of them green
> And some of them ripe! You ought to have seen!

Think about how many different kinds of descriptions of blueberries are in these seven lines: size (as big as the end of your thumb), color (sky-blue), weight (heavy), sound (ready to drum into a pail).

Now dictate the following lines to the student three times. Before you read, tell the student that you will read the lines only three times before asking her to write, and will not repeat them afterwards. Tell her that you will pause briefly at each comma, but that you will pause for a longer time at the end of the first line. Remind her that she should begin the second line right beneath the first line, and that the first word in each line is capitalized.

Be sure to indicate the exclamation point with an excited voice. You will also need to tell her that "sky-blue" is hyphenated.

Real sky-blue, and heavy, and ready to drum
In the cavernous pail of the first one to come!

Now ask the student to repeat the lines back to you before she writes. If she forgets, tell her to go back to the beginning of the lines and recite them again to jog her memory. If necessary, you may then prompt the student with single words.

Watch the student as she writes, and correct her at once if she begins to make a mistake.

Day Three: Poetry Exercise *Student pages 191–193*

***Focus:** Definitions of poetic terms*

Pull out Student page 191. Ask the student to write his name and the date. Do not allow the student to see Student page 192.

Allow the student to read the poem on Student page 191, either silently or aloud.

Tell the student that, instead of asking questions about the poem, you are going to discuss it with her.

Begin by asking the student whether the poem tells you who the Listeners are. You may allow her to try several explanations, but eventually you should tell her that the poem is deliberately mysterious. We don't know who the Listeners are! The poet, Walter de la Mare, doesn't *want* us to know. All we are supposed find out is that the Traveller had a promise to keep, and he kept it.

Now tell the student to assign a letter to each ending rhyme—but only the ending rhymes of *every other line*, where blanks are provided in the workbook. The first two blanks in the workbook are filled out already. (You may need to explain that "stone" and "gone" rhymed for the author, Walter de la Mare, because he had a British accent.)

Now, have the student check her answers against Student page 192.

Once the student has checked her answers, ask her to read the bolded words at the ends of the remaining lines on Student page 192: **Traveller, grasses, turret, time, Traveller, eyes, listeners, moonlight, stair, shaken, strangeness, turf, even, answered, listeners, house, stirrup, backward.** Ask her whether any of these words rhyme. She should answer that they do *not* rhyme. Tell the student that in this poem, rhymes happen only on every other line. This rhyme scheme gives the poet, Walter de la Mare, more freedom to choose words that will tell his story; he doesn't have to worry about finding a rhyme for the end of every line.

Finally, ask the student to read the poetic lines on Page 193, stressing each bolded syllable. When she is finished, point out that the patterns of **stress** unstress are different for every one of these lines. This poem isn't trochaic, or iambic. It isn't any other meter either. It has "uneven meter"—there is no single pattern of **stress** unstress.

When done, set the workbook page aside for the next lesson, which is on the back of it.

Day Four: Dictation Exercise *Student page 194*

Focus: *Poetic form, questions*

Pull out Student page 194. Ask the student to write her name and the date.

Tell the student that today's dictation exercise is from the poem "Will Ever?" by Walter de la Mare. Begin by reading the first two stanzas of the poem to the student:

Will he ever be weary of wandering,
 The flaming sun?
Ever weary of waning in lovelight,
 The white still moon?
Will ever a shepherd come
 With a crook of simple gold,
And lead all the little stars
 Like lambs to the fold?

Will ever the Wanderer sail
 From over the sea,
Up the river of water,
 To the stones to me?
Will he take us all into his ship,
 Dreaming, and waft us far,
To where in the clouds of the West
 The Islands are?

Now read the first four lines of the poem to the student, using your voice to emphasize the questions at the ends of the second and fourth lines:

Will he ever be weary of wandering,
 The flaming sun?
Ever weary of waning in lovelight,
 The white still moon?

Tell the student that you will dictate these lines to her three times. First, however, show the lines briefly to the student. Point out the commas at the ends of lines 1 and 3, and also point out that lines 2 and 4 are indented. Remind the student that each line begins with a capital letter.

Now remove the selection from the student's sight. Read these four lines three times, pausing significantly at the end of each line. Ask the student to repeat them back to you. If she cannot remember all four lines, repeat them additional times.

Watch the student as she writes, and correct her at once if she begins to make a mistake.

Day Five (optional): Creative Writing *Student page 195*

Pull out Student page 195. Write the student's name and the date for him as he watches, or ask him to write the name and date independently.

Instructor: Write a short poem about your favorite season. In your poem, answer at least two of the following questions: when you go outside during your favorite season, how does it feel? What do you see? What do you smell? What do you hear? What do you taste? If you like, draw a picture of yourself in your favorite season.

WEEK 22

Day One: Narration Exercise *Student pages 197–199*

***Focus:** Identifying the central theme in a selection*

Pull out Student pages 197–198 and 199. Ask the student to write his name and the date on Student page 199.

Allow the student to read the story on Student pages 197–198, either silently or aloud.

You will now ask the student to summarize the passage. This selection has a strong central theme which the student should identify. To guide him towards this type of summary, ask him, "In four sentences, tell me about Melvin's problem." His answer should resemble one of the following:

> "Melvin's father owned an ice cream factory, so all of Melvin's schoolmates came to his house to eat it. Melvin knew that his friends came over for the ice cream, so he told his father to give the ice cream away. Most of his friends stopped coming—until he started fixing bicycles. Then they all started bringing their broken chains for him to fix."

> "Melvin had a problem. His friends didn't like him for himself. At first, they came over to eat the ice cream from his father's factory. Then, they came over so he could fix their broken bicycles."

> "Melvin lived in a fancy house, and his father owned an ice cream factory. But Melvin knew that his friends only came over to eat ice cream, so he told his father to give it to orphans. Most of his friends stopped coming. But then Melvin started fixing bicycles, and his friends started coming again with their broken bicycle parts."

If the student has difficulty with this summary, say, "Try to tell me, in one sentence, what Melvin wanted his friends to do." The student should respond, "Melvin wanted his friends to like him for himself," OR "Melvin wanted his friends to come over because they liked him."

Once the student has come up with this sentence, say, "Now give me three more sentences with specific details in them about why Melvin's friends *actually* liked him, and how he reacted to them." The purpose of this exercise is to guide the student into stating the central theme of the passage and supporting that theme with specifics.

Write down the student's narration on Student page 199 as he watches.

When done, set the workbook page aside for the next lesson, which is on the back of it.

Day Two: Dictation Exercise *Student page 200*

Focus: *Prepositions*

Pull out Student page 200. Ask the student to write his name and the date.

Tell the student that today's dictation sentences are from another book by Jan Wahl, the author of *The Furious Flycycle.* Wahl wrote many other children's books. *Humphrey's Bear* is the story of a boy who dreams of his teddy bear coming to life and going on adventures with him. As the story begins, Humphrey's father has just said, "Isn't Humphrey getting a little too old to sleep with a teddy bear?"

Dictate the following sentences to the student three times. Before you read, tell the student that you will read the sentences only three times before asking him to write, and will not repeat them afterwards.

Pause at each comma, and indicate the end of the first sentence by allowing your voice to fall and pausing for a longer time. Do not warn the student ahead of time about the commas and periods.

> Humphrey didn't hear what his mom said. He just jumped under the blanket, snuggled with the brown bear, and slept.

Now ask the student to repeat the sentences back to you before he writes. If he forgets, tell him to go back to the beginning of the sentences and recite them again to jog his memory. If necessary, you may then prompt the student with single words.

Watch the student as he writes, and correct him at once if he begins to make a mistake.

When he is finished, tell him to circle the words "under" and "with" in the second sentence. Tell him that these words are *prepositions*—words that show the relationship between two different words. Who was under what? *He* was *under* the *blanket.* "Under" shows the relationship between "he" and the "blanket."

Who snuggled with what? *He* snuggled *with* the *bear.* "With" shows the relationship between "he" and the "bear."

Day Three: Narration and Dictation *Student pages 201–203*

Focus: *Identifying the central narrative thread in a passage and writing original sentences from dictation*

Pull out Student pages 201–202 and 203. Ask the student to write his name and the date on Student page 203.

Today's exercise will combine narration and dictation. Allow the student to read the story on Student pages 201–202, either silently or aloud.

You will now ask the student to summarize the passage. This selection lends itself to a narrative, story-like retelling. To guide the student towards this type of summary, say to him,

"In three or four sentences, what two important things happened in this passage?" His answer should resemble one of the following:

> "Melvin got very good at repairing things. He even fixed his father's ice cream freezer. His father was so grateful that he bought Melvin a beautiful silver bicycle. Then the great inventor Professor Mickimecki moved into town."
>
> "Melvin repaired his father's ice cream freezer when it broke down. His father bought him a Silver Zephyr bicycle, and Melvin rode it everywhere. Then a great inventor moved into town."
>
> "Melvin's father bought him a bicycle because Melvin fixed the freezer at the ice cream factory. Melvin rode the bicycle everywhere. Then a great inventor came to town. Melvin was very excited that the great inventor now lived in his town."

If the student has difficulty with this summary, ask the following four questions to help focus his thoughts:

> What did Melvin do for his father?
>
> What did his father do for him in return?
>
> Who moved to town?
>
> Why was this exciting for Melvin?

Then have the student repeat his answers in order; this will form his brief summary. Write down the student's narration on the lines below, but do not allow him to watch.

____

____

____

____

Then choose two or three sentences (16–20 words) to dictate back to the student. Repeat the sentences three times and ask the student to repeat them back to you before he writes on Student page 203.

Give all necessary help in spelling and punctuation.

When done, set the workbook page aside for the next lesson, which is on the back of it.

DAY FOUR: Dictation Exercise *Student page 204*

***Focus:** Prepositions, direct quotations*

Pull out Student page 204. Ask the student to write his name and the date.

Tell the student that today's dictation sentences are from *Humphrey's Bear* by Jan Wahl. Humphrey has fallen asleep now, and is dreaming about his teddy bear.

Dictate the following sentences to the student three times. Before you read, tell the student that these sentences have a direct quotation in them. Remind him that a direct quotation has quotation marks on either side of it. Also tell him that this direct quote ends with an exclamation point.

Pause at each comma, and indicate the end of the first sentence by allowing your voice to fall and pausing for a longer time. Be sure to use a different voice for the direct quotation "Get up!" and indicate the exclamation point by using an excited tone.

> As soon as Humphrey was asleep, the bear grew big, as it always did, and took him by the hand. "Get up!" called the bear, standing in the moonlight.

Now ask the student to repeat the sentences back to you before he writes. If he forgets, tell him to go back to the beginning of the sentences and recite them again to jog his memory. Since these sentences have a number of different elements in them (commas, periods, direct quotation, exclamation point), you may then repeat them additional times if necessary.

Watch the student as he writes, and correct him at once if he begins to make a mistake. You may need to remind him that "called" in the second sentence is not capitalized, because it does not begin a new sentence—it follows a direct quotation.

When he is finished, tell him to circle the word "in" in the second sentence. Remind him that this word is a *preposition*—a word that shows the relationship between two different words. The bear was standing in what? The *bear* was standing *in* the *moonlight.*

DAY FIVE (optional): Creative Writing *Student page 205*

Pull out Student page 205. Write the student's name and the date for her as she watches, or ask her to write the name and date independently.

> **Instructor:** If you could invent something to make your life easier, what would you invent? Here are some examples: an alarm clock that cooks your breakfast or a dinner plate that washes itself.

WEEK 23

Day One: Narration Exercise *Student pages 207–208*

***Focus:** Identifying the central narrative thread in a passage*

Pull out Student pages 207 and 208. Ask the student to write her name and the date on Student page 208.

Allow the student to read the story on Student page 207, either silently or aloud.

You will now ask the student to summarize the passage. This selection lends itself to a narrative, story-like retelling. To guide the student toward this type of summary, ask her, "In three or four sentences, tell me the story of Zeuxis and Parrhasius's competition." Her answer should resemble one of the following:

> "First, Zeuxis painted a picture of fruit that looked so real that birds came to peck at it. Then, Parrhasius painted curtains that were so real that Zeuxis tried to pull them aside. Finally, Zeuxis painted a picture of a boy carrying cherries. The birds tried to take the cherries, but they were not afraid of the boy."
>
> "Zeuxis painted a picture of fruit that looked so real that birds tried to peck at it. He said that he was the only person in the world who could paint so well. Then, Parrhasius painted a picture of curtains that even Zeuxis thought were real. Zeuxis said that he could only trick birds, but Parrhasius could trick a painter."
>
> "Zeuxis thought he was the best painter. Another painter named Parrhasius invited him over to look at a picture. Zeuxis asked Parrhasius to pull apart the curtains that were covering it. Parrhasius laughed because the curtain was the painting!"

If the student has difficulty with this summary, ask the following three questions to help focus her thoughts:

> Why was Zeuxis proud?
>
> What trick did Parrhasius play on Zeuxis?
>
> How did Zeuxis feel after seeing Parrhasius's painting?

The answers to these questions will make up the student's summary. Write the narration down on Student page 208 as the student watches.

Day Two: Dictation Exercise *Student page 209*

Focus: *Prepositions, objects of prepositions, prepositional phrases*

Pull out Student page 209. Tell the student that today's dictation sentence is adapted from "Two Great Painters" in *Fifty Famous People: A Book of Short Stories* by James Baldwin. The "he" in the sentence is Zeuxis, the ancient Greek painter who was proud of his ability to paint realistically.

Dictate the following sentence to the student three times. Before you read, tell the student that you will read the sentence only three times before asking her to write, and will not repeat it afterwards.

Pause significantly at the comma, but do not warn the student about the comma.

> One day, he painted a picture of some fruit which looked so real that the birds flew down and pecked at it.

Now ask the student to repeat the sentence back to you before she writes. If she forgets, tell her to go back to the beginning of the sentence and recite it again to jog her memory. If necessary, you may then prompt the student with single words.

Watch the student as she writes, and correct her at once if she begins to make a mistake.

When she is finished, tell her to circle the words "of" and "at." Tell her that these words are *prepositions*—words that show the relationship between two different words.

He painted a picture of what? *Of* some *fruit.* "Of" shows the relationship between "picture" and "fruit."

Birds flew down and pecked at what? Birds flew down and pecked *at it.* "At" shows the relationship between "pecked" and "it."

Tell the student to put a box around the words "fruit" and "it." Explain to her that these words are known as "objects of the preposition." The object of the preposition is the word that follows the preposition and answers the question "what?" Painted what? Painted *fruit.* Pecked at what? Pecked at *it.*

Ask the student to write the abbreviation "p." over each circled preposition, and "o.p." over each boxed object of the preposition.

Now tell the student to underline the words "of some fruit" and "at it." Explain to her that each set of words is a *prepositional phrase.* A prepositional phrase is made up of a preposition, its object, and any words (like "the" or "her") that modify the object. In the first prepositional phrase, "some" modifies the object "fruit."

Day Three: Narration and Dictation *Student pages 211–213*

Focus: *Identifying the central narrative thread in a passage and writing original sentences from dictation*

Pull out Student pages 211–212 and 213. Ask the student to write her name and the date on Student page 213.

Today's exercise will combine narration and dictation. Allow the student to read the story on Student pages 211–212, either silently or aloud.

Note to Instructor: You may need to explain that "congress" is a group of people who help make our country's laws. They vote on ideas for new laws (called *bills*) and decide how the government spends money.

You will now ask the student to summarize the passage. This selection lends itself to a narrative, story-like retelling. To guide the student towards this type of summary, say to the student, "In three or four sentences, tell me about what Samuel Morse needed to build his invention and how he got it."

"Mr. Morse was poor and needed money to build his invention. First, he sent letters to Congress to ask for help. Next, he travelled to Congress to ask again. When he had given up, Congress finally agreed to help."

"Mr. Morse became poor trying to build his invention. He traveled to Washington to ask for money from Congress. At first it seemed like nobody would help him. Then a senator's daughter ran into his hotel and told him that Congress said 'yes'!"

"At first, no one believed that Mr. Morse's invention would work. So he traveled to Washington to ask Congress for help. One night, he gave up. The next morning, a government official's daughter told him that Congress would help him."

If the student has difficulty with this summary, ask the following three questions to help focus her thoughts:

Why did Mr. Morse need help?

What did he do to try to get help?

What happened after he went to talk to Congress?

Then have the student repeat her answers in order; this will form her brief summary. Write down the student's narration on the lines below, but do not allow her to watch.

____

____

____

____

Then choose two or three sentences (16–20 words) to dictate back to the student. Repeat the sentences three times and ask the student to repeat them back to you before she writes on Student page 213.

Give all necessary help in spelling and punctuation.

When done, set the workbook page aside for the next lesson, which is on the back of it.

Day Four: Dictation Exercise *Student page 214*

Focus: *Prepositions, objects of prepositions, prepositional phrases*

Pull out Student page 214. Ask the student to write her name and the date.

Tell the student that today's dictation sentence is adapted from Samuel Morse's biography in *The Child's Book of American Biography* by Mary Stoyell Stimpson. The "he" in the sentences is Samuel Morse, trying to raise money to build his telegraph.

Dictate the following sentences to the student three times. Before you read, tell the student that you will read the sentences only three times before asking her to write, and will not repeat them afterwards.

Pause significantly at the periods, but do not tell the student how many periods are in the dictation exercise.

> He sent many letters to Congress asking for help.
> The men in Congress were not interested.

Now ask the student to repeat the sentences back to you before she writes. If she forgets, tell her to go back to the beginning of the sentences and recite them again to jog her memory. If necessary, you may then prompt the student with single words.

Watch the student as she writes, and correct her at once if she begins to make a mistake.

When she is finished, tell her to circle the word "to" in the first sentence and "in" in the second sentence. Tell her that these words are *prepositions*—words that show the relationship between two different words.

He sent many letters where? He *sent* many letters *to Congress.* "To" shows the relationship between "sent" and "Congress." The *men in Congress* were not interested. "In" shows the relationship between "men" and "Congress."

Tell the student to put boxes around the word "Congress" in both sentences. Ask her if she remembers what this word is called. If she cannot remember, explain to her that this word is the "object of the preposition." The object of the preposition is the word that follows the preposition and answers the question "what?" To *what*? To *Congress*. In what? In *Congress.*

Ask the student to write the abbreviation "p." over each circled preposition, and "o.p." over the boxed objects of the preposition.

Now tell the student to underline the words "to Congress" and "in Congress." Remind her that these are *prepositional phrases*. A prepositional phrase is made up of a preposition, its object, and any words that modify the object (these prepositional phrases do not happen to have any modifying words).

[Note: If you like, ask the student to find another prepositional phrase in these sentences—there is one more! If the student has trouble, you can tell her it is "for help." Then explain that "for help" is a prepositional phrase that explains *why* Samuel Morse asked. It shows the relationship between the verb "asked" and the noun "help."*]*

Day Five (optional): Creative Writing *Student page 215*

Pull out Student page 215. Write the student's name and the date for him as he watches, or ask him to write the name and date independently.

Instructor: This week we read about Parrhasius and Zeuxis, two talented painters. Tell me about one thing that you are good at or love to do.

WEEK 24

DAY ONE: Narration Exercise *Student pages 217–219*

Focus: *Identifying the central theme in a selection*

Pull out Student pages 217–218 and 219. Ask the student to write his name and the date on Student page 219.

Allow the student to read the story on Student pages 217–218, either silently or aloud.

You will now ask the student to summarize the passage. This selection has a strong central theme which the student should identify. To guide him towards this type of summary, say to the student, "Tell me, in one sentence, what obnoxious habit both Timmy and Wendy had." The student should respond with some variation of, "Timmy and Wendy were both tattletales." (If he says, "They were tattletales," encourage him to use the names of the children instead of the pronoun.)

Once the student has come up with this sentence, say, "Now give me two or three more sentences with specific details in them about *how* both Timmy and Wendy tell tales." The purpose of this exercise is to guide the student into stating the central theme of the passage and supporting that theme with specifics.

The answer should resemble one of the following:

> "Timmy and Wendy were both tattletales. Wendy told her teacher whenever anyone whispered, cheated, or wrote notes. Timmy told their mother that Wendy didn't eat her toast or wipe up Spot's water when she spilled it."

> "Timmy and Wendy were both tattletales. Wendy told on the other children in her class when they whispered or sucked their paintbrushes. She also told her mother that Timmy hadn't brushed his teeth and that he bought candy with his Sunday School money. Then Timmy told their mother that Wendy ate half the candy and that she spilled water and didn't wipe it up."

> "Timmy and Wendy were both tattletales. Wendy was a tattletale at school and at home. She told her teacher that Jimmy sucked on his paintbrush, and she told her mother that Timmy didn't brush his teeth or eat his liver. Then Timmy said that Wendy put her toast in the silverware drawer and ate half of his candy, and Wendy said that Timmy called her 'dog eyes.'"

If the student has difficulty with these details, ask these three questions:

> What did Wendy tattle about at school?
>
> What did Wendy tattle about at home?
>
> What did Timmy tell their mother about Wendy?

The answers to these questions will make up the rest of the student's summary.

Write the narration down on Student page 219 as the student watches.

When done, set the workbook page aside for the next lesson, which is on the back of it

DAY TWO: Dictation Exercise *Student page 220*

***Focus:** Adverbs that tell to what extent*

Pull out Student page 220. Ask the student to write his name and the date.

Tell the student that today's dictation sentence is from the story "The Tattletale Cure" in *Mrs. Piggle-Wiggle's Magic.* Mrs. Hamilton becomes so desperate that she calls Mrs. Piggle-Wiggle and asks her how to stop Timmy and Wendy from tattling. Mrs. Piggle-Wiggle has just the thing—special tattletale pills.

Now dictate the following sentences to the student three times. Before you read, tell the student that you will read the sentences only three times before asking him to write, and will not repeat them afterwards.

Indicate the end of the first sentence by allowing your voice to drop, but do not tell the student ahead of time that the selection contains two sentences.

> I do think we should start the tattletale cure right away. The pills look and taste just like licorice drops but the effect is quite remarkable.

Now ask the student to repeat the sentences back to you before he writes. If he forgets, tell him to go back to the beginning of the sentences and recite them again to jog his memory. If necessary, you may then prompt the student with single words.

Watch the student as he writes, and correct him at once if he begins to make a mistake.

When he is finished, tell him to circle the word "quite" in the second sentence. Tell him that this is an adverb. Remind him that an adverb is a word that modifies a verb, an adjective, or another adverb. It answers the questions "how, when, where, how often, to what extent?"

Ask the student what word "quite" modifies. If he is not sure, say, "The effect is quite what?" The answer is "remarkable."

Now ask the student to draw a line from the work "remarkable" back to the noun it describes. What is quite remarkable? The effect is quite remarkable. The line should point back to "effect."

Since "effect" is a noun, "remarkable" is an adjective. The adverb "quite" modifies an adjective.

Finally, ask the student which question this adverb answers: how, when, where, how often, to what extent? The answer is "to what extent." To what extent is the effect remarkable? It is *quite* remarkable.

Day Three: Narration and Dictation *Student pages 221–223*

Focus: *Identifying the central narrative thread in a passage and writing original sentences from dictation*

Pull out Student pages 221–222 and 223. Ask the student to write his name and the date on Student page 223.

Today's exercise will combine narration and dictation. Allow the student to read the story on Student pages 221–222, either silently or aloud.

You will now ask the student to summarize the passage. This selection lends itself to a narrative, story-like retelling. To guide the student towards this type of summary, ask him, "In three or four sentences, how did the magic pills begin to cure Wendy and Timmy?" His answer should resemble one of the following:

> "First, Wendy began to tell on Timmy, but a big puff of black smoke with little black tails on the bottom came out of her mouth instead. Then Timmy started to tattle, but a big puff of smoke with a tattletail on it came out of his mouth too. The next time they started to tell on each other, the same thing happened. So they stopped arguing and went out to shovel snow."

> "Whenever Wendy and Timmy started to tell on each other, big black puffs of smoke came out of their mouths. Each puff had a tail hanging on the bottom of it for each tattletale. Wendy and Timmy didn't want the puffs to come out of their mouths at school."

> "Wendy started to tell four tales about Timmy, and black smoke with four tails hanging from it came out of her mouth. Then Timmy started to tell a tale about Wendy, and black smoke with one tail came out of his mouth. Wendy decided that she would not want that to happen at school."

If the student has difficulty with this summary, ask the following three questions to help focus his thoughts:

> What happened when Wendy started to tell on Timmy?
>
> What happened when Timmy started to tell on Wendy?
>
> How did the children feel about this?

Then have the student repeat his answers in order; this will form his brief summary. Write down the student's narration on the lines below, but do not allow him to watch.

____

____

____

____

Then choose two or three sentences (16–20 words) to dictate back to the student. Repeat the sentences three times and ask the student to repeat them back to you before he writes on Student page 223.

Give all necessary help in spelling and punctuation.

When done, set the workbook page aside for the next lesson, which is on the back of it.

Day Four: Dictation Exercise *Student page 224*

Focus: *Adverbs that tell to what extent*

Pull out Student page 224. Ask the student to write his name and the date.

Tell the student that today's dictation sentences are also from "The Tattletale Cure."

Dictate the following sentences to the student three times. Before you read, tell the student that you will read the sentences only three times before asking him to write, and will not repeat them afterwards.

> During dinner the children were surprisingly quiet and surprisingly pleasant. In fact, there wasn't a cross word spoken the entire evening.

Now ask the student to repeat the sentences back to you before he writes. If he forgets, tell him to go back to the beginning of the sentences and recite them again to jog his memory. If necessary, you may then prompt the student with single words.

Watch the student as he writes, and correct him at once if he begins to make a mistake.

When he is finished, tell him to circle both occurrences of the word "surprisingly" in the first sentence. Tell him that these are adverbs that answer the question "to what extent?" Both adverbs modify adjectives. Ask the student to underline the adjectives that each adverb modifies. (The first modifies "quiet" and the second modifies "pleasant.").

Now ask the student to draw a line from "quiet" back to the noun that "quiet" modifies. Ask him to do the same with the adjective "pleasant." Both lines should point back to "children."

Day Five (optional): Creative Writing *Student page 225*

Pull out Student page 225. Write the student's name and the date for her as she watches, or ask her to write the name and date independently.

> **Instructor:** In the story, Mrs. Piggle-Wiggle gives Timmy and Wendy magic tattletale pills that force them to stop tattling. If you met Mrs. Piggle-Wiggle, what kind of magic pill would you ask her to make?

WEEK 25

Day One: Narration Exercise *Student pages 227–229*

***Focus:** Identifying the central details in a passage*

Pull out Student pages 227–228 and 229. Ask the student to write her name and the date on Student page 229.

Allow the student to read the story on Student pages 227–228, either silently or aloud.

You will now ask the student to summarize the passage. A detail-oriented summary is more appropriate to this descriptive passage than a summary telling what happens. Say to the student, "In three sentences, explain where at least three different names for money came from." The student can add details, but should not go over three sentences. Her answer should resemble one of the following:

> "The word 'money' comes from Moneta, one of the names of the Roman goddess Juno. The word 'coin' comes from the Latin word for 'wedge,' because the first coins were shaped like pieces of pie. The word 'cash' comes from the Chinese, but they borrowed it from the Portuguese."

> "The words 'money' and 'coin' both come from Latin, but the word 'dollar' comes from German. We call a dollar a 'buck' because North American Indians used to trade with buckskins. Germans call coins 'pinke-pinke' because the money jingles in your pocket."

> "The name for 'dollar' came from the German word 'thaler.' Spanish explorers brought this word to the Americas. 'Money' comes from a nickname of the goddess Juno, because the Romans made their money right next to Juno's temple."

If the student has trouble choosing important details, ask these three questions:

> What two money words come from Latin, and why?

> Where does the word "dollar" come from?

> Can you tell me two nicknames, or slang terms, for money?

The answers to these questions will make up the student's summary.

Write the narration down on Student page 229 as the student watches. (Note: put quotation marks around the money words that the student is describing, as shown above.)

When done, set the workbook page aside for the next lesson, which is on the back of it.

DAY TWO: Dictation Exercise *Student page 230*

***Focus:** Poetic form, titles of respect (abbreviations)*

Pull out Student page 230. Ask the student to write her name and the date.

Tell the student that today's dictation sentence is from another poem by Walter de la Mare, called "Miss T." Read the student the poem:

It's a very odd thing—
As odd as can be—
That whatever Miss T. eats
Turns into Miss T.;
Porridge and apples,
Mince, muffins and mutton,
Jam, junket, jumbles—
Not a rap, not a button
It matters; the moment
They're out of her plate,
Though shared by Miss Butcher
And sour Mr. Bate;
Tiny and cheerful,
And neat as can be,
Whatever Miss T. eats
Turns into Miss T.

Now tell the student that you will dictate the final six lines of the poem three times. The student should listen carefully to discover where each line ends and the next begins. Pause significantly at the end of each line.

Though shared by Miss Butcher
And sour Mr. Bate;
Tiny and cheerful,
And neat as can be,
Whatever Miss T. eats
Turns into Miss T.

Now ask the student to repeat the lines back to you before she writes. If she forgets, tell her to go back to the beginning of the lines and recite them again to jog her memory. If necessary, you may then repeat the lines additional times, until the student can remember all six.

Tell the student to stop writing at the end of each line and look up at you, so that you can tell her the proper punctuation for at each line's end.

Watch the student write and correct her at once if she begins to make a mistake. You may need to remind her that each poetic line begins right beneath the one above it. You may also need to prompt her to use capital letters for "Butcher" and "Bate," since these are proper names.

When she is finished, ask her to underline the titles of respect in the poem: "Miss" and "Mr." Beneath her dictation exercise, write out the word "Mister." Remind her that "Mr." is an abbreviation for "Mister," but that "Miss" is not abbreviated.

Day Three: Narration and Dictation *Student pages 231–232*

Focus: *Identifying the central details in a passage and writing original sentences from dictation*

Pull out Student pages 231 and 232. Ask the student to write her name and the date on Student page 232.

Today's exercise will combine narration and dictation. Allow the student to read the story on Student page 231, either silently or aloud.

You will now ask the student to summarize the passage. A detail-oriented summary is more appropriate to this descriptive passage than a summary telling what happens. Say to the student, "Tell me about three different kinds of coins described in this passage. Try to tell me when or where each coin was made. Try to use no more than four sentences." Her answer should resemble one of the following:

> "John Hull made coins with a date on one side and a tree on the other for the Massachusetts Bay colony. In the 1700s [or in the eighteenth century], many different colonies made copper coins. In 1878, James Jarvis made a coin called the Fugio cent. It was the first official United States coin."
>
> "It was easy for thieves to shave pieces off the edges of early coins like the New England pine tree coins. Most of the different colonies made copper coins—more than three hundred kinds. Finally James Jarvis made the first official United States coin. It said 'Time flies' on one side and 'Mind your business' on the other."
>
> "One of the first coins was the New England pine tree coin. Other colonies made their own coins. This got confusing, so Congress chose James Jarvis to make an official coin. It was called the Fugio cent."

If the student has trouble choosing important details, ask these three questions:

> What kind of coin did John Hull make in Massachusetts?
>
> What sort of coin did most of the colonies make for themselves?
>
> What was the first official United States coin like?

The answers to these questions will make up the student's summary.

Write down the student's narration on the lines below, but do not allow her to watch.

Then choose two or three sentences (16–20 words) to dictate back to the student. Repeat the sentences three times and ask the student to repeat them back to you before she writes on Student page 232.

Give all necessary help in spelling and punctuation.

Day Four: Dictation Exercise *Student page 233*

Focus: *Titles of respect (abbreviations)*

Pull out Student page 233. Ask the student to write her name and the date.

Tell the student that today's dictation sentences are a silly poem which was made up four hundred years ago. Here is the poem:

> I do not love thee, Dr. Fell,
> The reason why I cannot tell;
> But this I know, and know full well,
> I do not love thee, Dr. Fell.

Tell her that there is a story behind this poem. Dr. John Fell was the Bishop of Oxford over three hundred years ago. It was part of his job to expel students (force them to leave university) if they didn't study or follow the rules.

One student who had a hard time studying and following the rules was a young man named Tom Brown. Dr. Fell was ready to expel Tom Brown, but he gave Tom one chance to stay in school. He told Tom that he could remain at Oxford if he could translate, on the spot, a Latin poem written by the Latin poet Martial.

Martial's poem is written to one of his ancient enemies, a man named Sabidius. The poem goes like this: "Non amo te, Sabidi, nec possum dicere - quare; Hoc tantum possum dicere, non amo te." (It's OK to simply pronounce all of the Latin words as though they are English words.)

In English, the poem means something like, "I don't like you, Sabidius, and I can't say why. But I can say this: I don't like you."

Tom Brown was a quick thinker. He immediately answered,

I do not love thee, Dr. Fell,
The reason why I cannot tell;
But this I know, and know full well,
I do not love thee, Dr. Fell.

Dr. Fell was amused, and he let Tom Brown stay in school.

After explaining the poem, read it three more times to the student, pausing significantly at the commas within the lines. You may need to repeat it additional times. When the student can repeat it back to you, tell her to begin to write. She should look up at the end of every line so that you can tell her the correct punctuation.

Watch the student write and correct her at once if she begins to make a mistake. You may need to remind her that each poetic line begins right beneath the one above it.

When she is finished, ask her to underline the title of respect in the poem: "Dr." Beneath her dictation exercise, write out the word "Doctor." Remind her that "Dr." is an abbreviation for "Doctor."

When done, set the workbook page aside for the next lesson, which is on the back of it.

Day Five (optional): Creative Writing *Student page 234*

Pull out Student page 234. Write the student's name and the date for him as he watches, or ask him to write the name and date independently.

> **Instructor:** Kings and queens of old had coins made with their faces, scenes from their lives, or their greatest accomplishments stamped onto them. If you had a coin designed to celebrate you, what would you put on it? If you like, draw a picture of your coin based on your written description.

WEEK 26

Day One: Narration Exercise *Student pages 235–237*

***Focus:** Identifying the central narrative thread in a passage*

Pull out Student pages 235–236 and 237. Ask the student to write his name and the date on Student page 237.

Allow the student to read the story on Student pages 235–236, either silently or aloud.

You will now ask the student to summarize the passage. This selection lends itself to a narrative, story-like retelling. To guide the student towards this type of summary, say to him, "In three or four sentences, tell me what happened when Babe met Fly and her puppies." His answer should resemble one of the following:

> "Fly and her puppies looked over into the loose box and saw Babe. The puppies said that Babe was stupid, but Fly was kind to the little pig. She asked him his name and said that she would take care of him from now on."
>
> "Farmer Hogget put his new piglet in a loose box. The puppies and Fly looked down at the piglet and Fly asked the piglet his name. He said that his name was Babe, and he missed his mother. Fly said that she would look after him."
>
> "When Fly and her puppies saw Babe in the barn, the puppies started to make fun of him. But Fly felt sorry for the piglet. She sent her puppies to play in the yard, and then jumped down to take care of Babe. She told him that she would look after him."

If the student has difficulty with this summary, ask the following four questions to help focus his thoughts:

> Where was the piglet when Fly and her puppies first saw him?
>
> How did the puppies react to the piglet?
>
> How did Fly feel when she saw that Babe was unhappy?
>
> What did she promise?

The answers to these questions will make up the student's summary.

Write the narration down on Student page 237 as the student watches.

When done, set the workbook page aside for the next lesson, which is on the back of it.

Day Two: Dictation Exercise *Student page 238*

***Focus:** Abbreviations for months and days of the week*

Pull out Student page 238. Ask the student to write his name and the date.

Tell the student that today's dictation sentences give more information about Dick King-Smith, the author of *Babe: The Gallant Pig* and many other books about animals.

Dictate the following sentences to the student three times. Before you read, tell the student that he should abbreviate the month of March. You will read "March," but he should write the abbreviation instead. Also tell him that there is a hyphen between "King" and "Smith."

When you read, indicate the commas in the second and third sentence by pausing. Indicate the end of each sentence by pausing for a longer time, and by allowing your voice to fall slightly. Do not tell the student ahead of time that there will be three separate sentences.

Now tell the student that you will read the sentences four times before asking him to write, and will not repeat them afterwards. (Since there are three sentences, an extra repetition is appropriate.)

> Dick King-Smith was born Mar. 27, 1922. For twenty years, he worked as a farmer in England. When he began to write for children, he often told stories about farm animals.

Now ask the student to repeat the sentences back to you before he writes. If he forgets, tell him to go back to the beginning of the sentences and recite them again to jog his memory. If necessary, you may then prompt the student with single words.

Watch the student as he writes, and correct him at once if he begins to make a mistake.

Day Three: Narration and Dictation *Student pages 239–241*

***Focus:** Identifying the central details in a passage and writing original sentences from dictation*

Pull out Student pages 239–240 and 241. Ask the student to write his name and the date on Student page 241.

Today's exercise will combine narration and dictation. Allow the student to read the story on Student pages 239–240, either silently or aloud.

You will now ask the student to summarize the passage. A detail-oriented summary is more appropriate to this descriptive passage than a summary telling what happens. Say to the student, "Describe what the sheep was like, from Babe's point of view, in three sentences." His answer should resemble one of the following:

> "The sheep was stamping her foot and complaining about wolves. She told Babe she was a ewe, and Babe thought she was stupid. He also thought that her name was Ma."
>
> "The sheep thought that Babe was a wolf until she saw him. She told him that her name was Ma, and that she had foot rot and a cough. Then she burped and started to chew her cud."
>
> "At first, the sheep thought that Babe was a wolf. She told him that she was a ewe, and that her name was Ma. She had a cough and foot rot, and she was chewing her cud."

If the student has trouble choosing important details, ask these three questions:

What did the sheep think of Babe, at first?

What two names did Babe learn for the sheep?

What was wrong with the sheep?

Then have the student repeat his answers in order; this will form his brief summary. Write down the student's narration on the lines below, but do not allow him to watch.

____

____

____

____

Then choose two or three sentences (16–20 words) to dictate back to the student. Repeat the sentences three times and ask the student to repeat them back to you before he writes on Student page 241.

Give all necessary help in spelling and punctuation.

When done, set the workbook page aside for the next lesson, which is on the back of it.

DAY FOUR: Dictation Exercise *Student page 242*

Focus: *Abbreviations for months and days of the week*

Pull out Student page 242. Ask the student to write his name and the date.

Dictate the following sentences to the student three times. Before you read, tell the student that he should use the abbreviations for "Saturday" and "October," even though you will read the entire words as you dictate. Tell the student that "Cinderella May" is two separate words making up the dog's full name, so both should be capitalized. Also tell him that the sentences contain the words "68 inches"; he should write 68 inches with the *numeral* "68" and the *word* "inches."

When you read the sentences, pause significantly at each comma. Make a longer pause at the period and indicate the end of the first sentence by allowing your voice to fall. Do not tell the student how many commas or sentences are in the selection.

Now tell the student that you will read the sentences only four times before asking him to write, and will not repeat them afterwards. (Since the student will need to keep several different things in mind as he listens, an extra repetition is appropriate.)

> On Sat., Oct. 7, 2006, a dog named Cinderella May jumped higher than any other dog in the world. Cinderella May cleared a wooden rail set at 68 inches, which is over five feet high.

Now ask the student to repeat the sentences back to you before he writes. If he forgets, tell him to go back to the beginning of the sentences and recite them again to jog his memory. If necessary, you may then prompt the student with single words.

Watch the student as he writes, and correct him at once if he begins to make a mistake.

Day Five (optional): Creative Writing *Student page 243*

Pull out Student page 243. Write the student's name and the date for her as she watches, or ask her to write the name and date independently.

Instructor: Complete the story below by adding 1-2 sentences:

I woke up because something was scratching me. I was lying in a bed of straw. "Where am I? Where is my bed?" I wondered. Then I saw my reflection in a pane of glass lying in the barn . . . "I am a pig!" . . .

If you like, draw an illustration to accompany your story.

WEEK 27

Day One: Narration Exercise *Student pages 245–246*

***Focus:** Identifying the central theme in a selection*

Pull out Student pages 245 and 246. Ask the student to write her name and the date on Student page 246.

Allow the student to read the passage on Student page 245, either silently or aloud.

You will now ask the student to summarize the passage. This selection has a strong central theme which the student should identify. To guide her towards this type of summary, say to her, "Tell me in one sentence what border collies are good at." The student should respond, "Border collies are good at driving animals," OR "Border collies are good at gathering animals together and herding them towards a farmer," OR "Border collies are good at obeying commands and working on farms."

Once the student has come up with this sentence, say, "Now give me two or three more sentences with specific details in them about what border collies do." The purpose of this exercise is to guide the student into stating the central theme of the passage and supporting that theme with specifics.

The answer should resemble one of the following:

> "Border collies are good at driving animals. They gather sheep together by glaring at them, and they have an instinct that helps them drive animals towards farmers. They can work out of sight of the farmer, and they can understand twenty different commands."
>
> "Border collies are good at gathering animals together and herding them towards a farmer. They crouch down and glare at sheep to make them obey. They can also be taught to drive a herd of animals away from a farmer."
>
> "Border collies are good at obeying commands and working on farms. They naturally drive animals towards a farmer, and they can also learn to drive animals away. They can understand nearly twenty different commands. They can even learn to solve problems by themselves when the farmer is not there."

If the student has difficulty with this summary, ask the following three questions to help focus his thoughts.

> What do border collies naturally do?
>
> What can border collies learn to do, with some practice?
>
> How many commands can a border collie understand?

The answers to these questions will make up the student's summary.

Write the narration down on Student page 246 as the student watches.

Day Two: Dictation Exercse *Student page 247*

***Focus:** Commas in a series*

Pull out Student page 247. Ask the student to write her name and the date.

Tell the student that today's dictation sentences are from the book *Border Collies* by Michael DeVine. Before you give the dictation sentences, you will read a paragraph from the book to give the student some background.

Here is what the book says about border collies and the way they herd sheep: "Modern border collies are typified by a working style that involves a quiet, head-down style that is remarkably similar to a wolf creeping up on its prey. Instead of barking and nipping excessively, border collies use 'eye.' A border collie with strong 'eye' will stare at bunched stock until they decide there are better places to be. Some people are even a little put off by the breed's tendency to stare at them."

The book then describes several famous border collies who won prizes for herding sheep and cattle, and who all won the highest prize for border collies: the International Supreme Championship.

Now dictate the following sentences to the student three times. Before you read, tell the student that you will read the sentences only three times before asking her to write, and will not repeat them afterwards.

Pause significantly at each comma. Indicate the end of the first sentence by allowing your voice to fall and pausing for a slightly longer time.

> These dogs ranged greatly in size, color, and hair coat. But they shared extreme intelligence, instinctive stock sense, and a quiet working style.

Now ask the student to repeat the sentences back to you before she writes. If she forgets, tell her to go back to the beginning of the sentences and recite them again to jog her memory. If necessary, you may then prompt the student with single words.

Watch the student as she writes, and correct her at once if she begins to make a mistake. Be sure to remind her to insert the commas.

When the student is finished writing, ask her to underline "size," "color," and "hair coat" in the first sentence. Tell her that this is a list, or series, of items. The items are the three ways in which the dogs were different. When there are more than two items in a series, the items should be separated by commas.

Now ask her to underline the words "intelligence," "stock sense," and "working style" in the second sentence. (You may need to explain that "stock sense" is an instinct that allows the dog to guess what an animal is about to do.) Tell her that this is also a list, or series. In this list, the items are the ways in which the dogs were alike. Because there are three items, they are separated by commas.

Day Three: Narration and Dictation *Student pages 249–250*

Focus: *Summarizing a series of ordered facts and writing original sentences from dictation*

Pull out Student pages 249 and 250. Ask the student to write her name and the date on Student page 250.

Today's exercise will combine narration and dictation. Allow the student to read the passage on Student page 249, either silently or aloud.

You will now ask the student to summarize the passage. This passage lists a series of ordered steps. The student doesn't need to remember all six phases of the sheepdog trial in order! Instead, ask her to look at the six phases listed on Student page 250. While looking at these phases, the student should summarize the trial in four or five sentences, keeping the phases in their correct order. Tell her that she does not need to use the name of the phases; instead she should describe what the dog is doing, in order, and add a few details about what the sheep and the handler are doing as well.

She should attempt to do this without looking back at the passage, but if necessary you may allow her to glance at Student page 201. This is a difficult exercise, so give whatever help is necessary.

Her answer should resemble one of the following:

> "The dog leaves the post and contacts the sheep so he can bring them back to the handler. He is supposed to drive them in a straight line, but the sheep like to wander off. Then the dog herds the sheep through gates. Next, he cuts two sheep with special collars off from the flock. Then he herds all the sheep into a pen."
>
> "The dog leaves the post, contacts the sheep, and brings them back to the handler. Then he herds the sheep through special gates, without upsetting them. He cuts off two special sheep from the rest, and then herds all the sheep into a pen. The handler can try to keep the sheep from wandering off, but he can't let go of the gate."
>
> "First, the dog leaves the post. He circles around to the right or left of the sheep to make contact with them. He herds them back to the handler in a straight line. Then the dog herds them through gates, cuts two sheep off from the rest, and then drives them into the pen. The sheep do not like to go in straight lines, and they keep trying to wander off and turn the wrong way."

Write down the student's narration on the lines below, but do not allow her to watch.

____

____

____

____

Then choose two or three sentences (16–20 words) to dictate back to the student. Repeat the sentences three times and ask the student to repeat them back to you before she writes on Student page 250.

Give all necessary help in spelling and punctuation.

Day Four: Dictation Exercise *Student page 251*

***Focus:** Commas in a series*

Pull out Student page 251. Ask the student to write her name and the date.

Tell the student that today's dictation sentences are based on information found in *The Shetland Sheepdog,* by Charlotte Wilcox.

Dictate the following sentences to the student three times. Before you read, tell the student that you will read the sentences only three times before asking her to write, and will not repeat them afterwards.

Be sure to pause significantly at each comma. Indicate the end of the first sentence by allowing your voice to fall and pausing for a longer time. Indicate the exclamation point at the end of the second sentence by using an excited voice. After you read the sentences the first time, ask the student if she noticed your excited voice. Ask her what punctuation mark shows excitement.

Then complete the dictation by reading the sentences twice more in the same way.

> Sheepdogs are loyal, intelligent, and good with children. Some sheepdogs actually herd children together into groups to keep them safe as they play!

Now ask the student to repeat the sentences back to you before she writes. If she forgets, tell her to go back to the beginning of the sentences and recite them again to jog her memory. If necessary, you may then prompt the student with single words.

Watch the student as she writes, and correct her at once if she begins to make a mistake. Be sure to remind her to insert the commas and exclamation point.

When the student is finished writing, ask her to underline "loyal," "intelligent," and "good with children" in the first sentence. Tell her that this is a list, or series, of items. The items are the three qualities of sheepdogs. When there are more than two items in a series, the items should be separated by commas.

When done, set the workbook page aside for the next lesson, which is on the back of it.

Day Five (optional): Creative Writing *Student page 252*

Pull out Student page 252. Write the student's name and the date for him as he watches, or ask him to write the name and date independently.

> **Instructor:** If you had a pet dog (or any other pet), what cool trick would you want to teach them? If you like, add details to the picture of the border collie on Student Page 252. You could draw the dog a special treat or toy for doing a great job, or give the dog a beautiful collar.

WEEK 28

Day One: Narration Exercise *Student pages 253–255*

***Focus:** Identifying the central narrative thread in a passage*

Pull out Student pages 253–254 and 255. Ask the student to write his name and the date on Student page 255.

Allow the student to read the story on Student pages 253–254, either silently or aloud.

You will now ask the student to summarize the passage. This selection lends itself to a narrative, story-like retelling. To guide the student towards this type of summary, ask him, "In three sentences, what happened when Marilla and Anne met each other?" His answer should resemble one of the following:

> "Marilla was surprised to see that Matthew had brought home a girl. The little girl realized that she wasn't wanted, and burst into tears. Marilla told her not to cry, and asked her what her name was."
>
> "When Matthew and Anne came into the house, Marilla asked where the boy was. Anne began to cry because no one wanted her, and Marilla asked what her name was. Anne asked Marilla to call her Cordelia, but Marilla said that Anne was a good plain name."
>
> "Matthew told Marilla that he had to bring Anne home even though she was a girl. Anne realized that she wasn't supposed to be there, and began to cry. But Marilla told her that she could stay while they found out what the mistake was."

If the student has difficulty with this summary, ask the following three questions to help focus his thoughts:

> What was Marilla's reaction when she saw Anne?
>
> What did Anne do when she realized that there had been a mistake?
>
> When Anne began to cry, how did Marilla respond?

The answers to these questions will make up the student's summary.

Write the narration down on Student page 255 as the student watches.

When done, set the workbook page aside for the next lesson, which is on the back of it.

Day Two: Dictation Exercise *Student page 256*

***Focus:** Ending exclamation points*

Pull out Student page 256. Ask the student to write his name and the date.

Tell the student that today's dictation sentence is from Chapter One of *Anne of Green Gables,* "Mrs. Rachel Lynde Is Surprised." Mrs. Rachel Lynde, the Cuthberts' nosy neighbor, has just found out that Marilla and Matthew have sent to the orphanage for a boy.

Dictate the following sentences to the student three times. Before you read, tell the student that you will read the sentences only three times before asking him to write, and will not repeat them afterwards.

Before you read, tell the student that there are two exclamation points in the selection; indicate them with your voice while you read. You may also want to point out that the last two sentences are fragments; this is an appropriate use of a fragment in writing.

> Mrs. Rachel felt that she had received a severe mental jolt. She thought in exclamation points. A boy! Marilla and Matthew Cuthbert of all people adopting a boy!

Now ask the student to repeat the sentences back to you before he writes. If he forgets, tell him to go back to the beginning of the sentences and recite them again to jog his memory. If necessary, you may then prompt the student with single words.

Watch the student as he writes, and correct him at once if he begins to make a mistake. You may need to help him spell "Marilla," "Matthew," and "Cuthbert." If necessary, remind him that "Mrs." is an abbreviation for a married woman.

Day Three: Narration and Original Sentence Exercise *Student pages 257–259*

***Focus:** Identifying the central details in a passage and writing original sentences*

Pull out Student pages 257–258 and 259. Ask the student to write his name and the date on Student page 259.

Today's exercise will require the student to write an original sentence. Allow the student to read the story on Student pages 257–258, either silently or aloud. Before he reads, tell him that you will be asking him to describe Prince Edward Island in his summary (although he certainly does not need to remember every detail!).

You will now ask the student to summarize the passage. To guide him towards a detail-oriented summary, say, "Describe Prince Edward Island in two or three sentences. Be sure to use specific names for trees, plants, and animals." His answer should resemble one of the following:

> "Prince Edward Island has pines, willows, maples, and many other trees. The island also has strawberries, raspberries, grain, and peas. There are many pigeons in the forests."
>
> "The forests on Prince Edward Island are many different colors of green because there are so many different trees—like pines, elms, and beeches. The island is pleasant and warm, and there are gooseberries, strawberries, peas, and raspberries growing there."
>
> "Jacques Cartier sailed to the north end of Prince Edward Island and described it. He said that there were many different trees, such as pines and maples, and wild berries, like strawberries and raspberries."

If the student has trouble choosing important details, ask these three questions:

> Name three trees that were in the forests.
>
> Name three foods that grew in the meadows and forests.
>
> Can you remember one more thing about the island?

(If the student draws a blank, ask him what the weather was like, whether there were any birds, or which explorer landed on it.)

Write down the student's narration on the lines below, but do not allow him to watch.

____

____

____

____

Now ask him whether he can repeat the first sentence of the narration to himself. If not, read him the first sentence of the narration only. Tell him to listen carefully, since you will only read it once. Encourage him to repeat it to himself until he can remember it, and then to say it out loud to himself as he writes it down on Student page 259.

Give all necessary help in spelling and punctuation.

When done, set the workbook page aside for the next lesson, which is on the back of it.

Day Four: Dictation Exercise — *Student page 260*

Focus: *Ending question marks*

Pull out Student page 260. Ask the student to write his name and the date.

Tell the student that today's dictation sentences are also from *Anne of Green Gables.*

Explain that although Prince Edward Island is cold in the winter, Jacques Cartier landed on the island in midsummer. Anne also arrived at the Cuthbert farm in summer. This selection from Chapter Four, "Morning at Green Gables," describes when she first looked out of her window.

Dictate the following sentences to the student three times. Before you read, tell the student that you will read the sentences only three times before asking her to write, and will not repeat them afterwards.

Be sure to indicate the period by pausing. Tell the student before you read that there are two question marks in the selection, and use a questioning voice for the two questions at the end.

> Anne dropped on her knees and gazed out into the June morning, her eyes glistening with delight. Oh, wasn't it beautiful? Wasn't it a lovely place?

Now ask the student to repeat the sentences back to you before he writes. If he forgets, tell him to go back to the beginning of the sentences and recite them again to jog his memory. If necessary, you may then prompt the student with single words.

Watch the student as he writes on Student page 260, and correct him at once if he begins to make a mistake. You may need to remind him that "wasn't" is a contraction and has an apostrophe between the last two letters.

Day Five (optional): Creative Writing *Student page 261*

Pull out Student page 261. Write the student's name and the date for her as she watches, or ask her to write the name and date independently.

> **Instructor:** What is your favorite place to be in the whole world? Describe it. In your response, answer at least one of the following questions: Where is your favorite place? What does it look like in your favorite place? What does it smell like? What does it feel like to be there? What can you do there?

WEEK 29

DAY ONE: Narration Exercise — *Student pages 263–265*

***Focus:** Identifying the central details in a passage*

Pull out Student pages 263–264 and 265. Ask the student to write her name and the date on Student page 265.

Allow the student to read the story on Student pages 263–264, either silently or aloud.

You will now ask the student to summarize the passage. A detail-oriented summary is more appropriate to this descriptive passage than a summary telling what happens. Use a "directed narration starter": say to the student, "Describe the Britons in three sentences." Her answer should resemble one of the following:

> "The Britons were tall men with red hair and plaid clothes. They lived in houses that were piles of stones. The men hunted wild boars, the women raised corn, and they had fortresses in the woods built out of tree trunks."
>
> "Julius Caesar tried to conquer the Britons. He found out that they lived in houses of stone, with strong places made out of tree trunks. He couldn't conquer these, but he made the Britons give him pearls and call the Romans their masters."
>
> "The Britons had long red streaming hair and fought the Romans with darts. They hunted boars, wolves, and stags, grew corn for bread, and spun wool into clothes. Caesar forced them to pay tribute."

If the student has trouble choosing important details, ask these three questions:

> What were the men of the Britons like?
>
> What did the men and women do for food?
>
> What did Caesar force the Britons to do?

The answers to these questions will make up the student's summary.

Write the narration down on Student page 265 as the student watches.

When done, set the workbook page aside for the next lesson, which is on the back of it.

DAY TWO: Dictation Exercise — *Student page 266*

***Focus:** Commas in direct address*

Pull out Student page 266. Ask the student to write her name and the date.

Tell the student that today's dictation sentences are from *Julius Caesar* by William Shakespeare. In Shakespeare's famous play about Caesar, the Roman soldier Mark Antony gives a funeral oration, or speech, after Caesar's death. The dictation sentences are the first two lines of that oration. Tell the student that the sentences are poetry: each sentence begins a new line.

Now dictate the following sentence to the student three times. Before you read, tell the student that you will read the sentences only three times before asking her to write, and will not repeat them afterwards.

Be sure to pause at each comma; pause for a longer time at the end of the first line, and indicate the end of the sentence by allowing your voice to drop.

> Friends, Romans, countrymen, lend me your ears.
> I come to bury Caesar, not to praise him.

Now ask the student to repeat the sentences back to you before she writes. If she forgets, tell her to go back to the beginning of the sentences and recite them again to jog her memory. If necessary, you may then prompt the student with single words.

You may need to remind her that the second line of poetry begins immediately beneath the first; you will probably also need to help her spell "Caesar." If necessary, remind her that "Caesar" and "Romans" are both proper names and should be capitalized.

Watch the student as she writes, and correct her at once if she begins to make a mistake. When she is finished writing, ask her to read the words "Friends, Romans, countrymen" out loud. Tell her that all three of these are words of direct address: they are words that *name* the people to whom the speaker is talking.

Ask the student to circle the commas after "Friends," "Romans," and "countrymen." Tell her that words of direct address should be followed by commas.

Day Three: Narration and Original Sentence Exercise *Student pages 267–269*

***Focus:** Identifying the central theme in a selection and writing original sentences*

Pull out Student pages 267–268 and 269. Ask the student to write her name and the date on Student page 269.

Today's exercise will require the student to write an original sentence. Allow the student to read the story on Student pages 267–268, either silently or aloud.

You will now ask the student to summarize the passage. This selection has a central theme which the student should identify. To guide the student towards this type of summary, say to her, "Tell me in one sentence what happened to the Britons." The student should respond, "The Britons were driven into Wales," OR "The Britons were driven into the north and west of Britain," OR, "The Angles took Britain away from the Britons."

Once the student has come up with this sentence, say, "Now give me three more sentences with specific details in them about how this happened to the Britons. Be sure to mention the Romans and the Angles." The purpose of this exercise is to guide the student into stating the central theme of the passage and supporting that theme with specifics.

The answer should resemble one of the following:

> "The Britons were driven into Wales. First, the Romans lived in Britain for four hundred years. Then the Angles came across the North Sea and took Britain. Now Britain is called England."
>
> "The Britons were driven into the north and west of Britain. The Romans had taken Britain and built roads and towns for themselves. But then tall, blue-eyed men called Angles came over the ocean and fought against the Romans. They took Britain for themselves."
>
> "The Angles took Britain away from the Britons. First, the Romans lived in England. Then the Angles invaded and fought against the Romans and the Britons. King Arthur fought against the Angles, but he could not drive them away."

If the student has difficulty with this summary, ask the following three questions to help focus her thoughts:

> How long did the Romans live in Britain?
>
> Who arrived in Britain next?
>
> What did these invaders do to the British?

Then have the student repeat her answers in order; this will form her brief summary. Write down the student's narration on the lines below, but do not allow her to watch.

____

____

____

____

Now ask her whether she can repeat the first sentence of the narration to herself. If not, read her the first sentence of the narration only. Tell her to listen carefully, since you will only read it once. Encourage her to repeat it to herself until she can remember it, and then to say it out loud to herself as he writes it down on Student page 269.

Give all necessary help in spelling and punctuation.

When done, set the workbook page aside for the next lesson, which is on the back of it.

DAY FOUR: Dictation Exercise *Student page 270*

***Focus:** Commas in direct address*

Pull out Student page 270. Ask the student to write her name and the date.

Tell the student that today's dictation sentences are from the story of King Arthur. These are the words that Arthur spoke as he lay dying to his friend, a knight named Bedivere.

Dictate the following sentences to the student three times. Before you read, tell the student that you will read the sentences only three times before asking her to write, and will not repeat them afterwards.

Remind the student that Arthur's words should have quotation marks around them. Pause at each comma; indicate the end of the first sentence by pausing for a slightly longer time and allowing your voice to fall. Be sure to use a slightly different voice for Arthur's exact words.

> Arthur said, "Take the sword, good knight, and throw it into the water. Then come back and tell me what you see."

Now ask the student to repeat the sentences back to you before she writes. If she forgets, tell her to go back to the beginning of the sentences and recite them again to jog her memory. If necessary, you may then prompt the student with single words.

Watch the student as she writes, and correct her at once if she begins to make a mistake.

When she is finished writing, ask her to read the words "good knight" out loud. Tell her that these words *name* the friend to whom Arthur is speaking. They are words of direct address.

Ask the student to circle the commas before and after "good knight." Tell her that words of direct address should be surrounded by commas when they come in the middle of a sentence.

Day Five (optional): Creative Writing *Student page 271*

Pull out Student page 271. Write the student's name and the date for him as he watches, or ask him to write the name and date independently.

> **Instructor:** Listen as I read the description of the Britons on Student pages 263–264. Using the description you just heard, complete the illustration on Student pages 271? You will need crayons or something to color with! If you like, write a sentence describing what chore you might have if you grew up in a family of ancient Britons.

WEEK 30

Day One: Narration Exercise *Student pages 273–275*

***Focus:** Identifying the central narrative thread in a passage*

Pull out Student pages 273–274 and 275. Ask the student to write his name and the date on Student page 275.

Allow the student to read the story on Student pages 273–274, either silently or aloud.

You will now ask the student to summarize the passage. This selection lends itself to a narrative, story-like retelling. To guide the student towards this type of summary, say to him, "Tell me in three or four sentences how Alec fell off the ship and was rescued by the Black." His answer should resemble one of the following:

> "The Black knocked Alec off the ship just before it sank. There were no lifeboats, but he grabbed onto the rope attached to the Black's halter. The Black pulled him through the water all night."
>
> "Alec went to let the Black out, and the horse knocked him off the ship and into the water. When he came up, he saw the ship sinking. The Black swam by him, and Alec grabbed the horse's rope. He tied it to his waist so that the Black could tow him through the water."
>
> "The Black leaped off the ship and knocked Alec into the water. Alec grabbed the rope attached to the Black's halter and tied it to his waist. The horse pulled him through the water until they got close to land."

If the student has difficulty with this summary, ask the following three questions to help focus his thoughts:

> What made Alec fall off the ship?
>
> What did he grab to save him?
>
> What did the Black do for the next few hours?

The answers to these questions will make up the student's summary.

Write the narration down on Student page 275 as the student watches.

When done, set the workbook page aside for the next lesson, which is on the back of it.

Day Two: Dictation Exercise *Student page 276*

***Focus:** Contractions*

Pull out Student page 276. Ask the student to write his name and the date.

Tell the student that today's dictation sentences are also from *The Black Stallion*. The Black tows Alec to an island, where the boy and horse are marooned together. In these sentences, Alec tries to figure out how to survive.

Dictate the following sentences to the student three times. Before you read, tell the student that you will read the sentences only three times before asking him to write, and will not repeat them afterwards.

Be sure to indicate the exclamation point with an excited voice. Pause briefly at both commas.

You may need to remind the student that "Black" is capitalized because it is the horse's proper name.

> He wasn't licked yet! He'd find some way to make a shelter, and if that wasn't possible, then he'd sleep outside like the Black.

Now ask the student to repeat the sentences back to you before he writes. If he forgets, tell him to go back to the beginning of the sentences and recite them again to jog his memory. If necessary, you may then prompt the student with single words.

Watch the student as he writes, and correct him at once if he begins to make a mistake.

When he is finished, ask him to find and underline the four contractions in the sentences. He should underline both occurrences of "wasn't" and "he'd." Ask him to write the contracted words out in full beneath his dictation. He should write "was not" and "he would." Point out that in the contraction "he'd," four letters drop out!

Day Three: Narration and Original Sentence Dictation *Student pages 277–279*

***Focus:** Identifying the central narrative thread in a passage and writing original sentences*

Pull out Student pages 277–278 and 279. Ask the student to write his name and the date on Student page 279.

Today's exercise will require the student to write an original sentence. Allow the student to read the story on Student pages 277–278, either silently or aloud.

You will now ask the student to summarize the passage. This selection lends itself to a narrative, story-like retelling. To guide the student towards this type of summary, say to him, "In three or four sentences, tell me how Alec finally got onto the Black and rode him. Be sure to also tell me what the ride was like, and how it ended." His answer should resemble one of the following:

"At first, the Black bucked Alec off. But then Alec got onto his back and the Black broke into a run. The Black galloped through a ravine and jumped over a gully. Finally the Black slowed down and Alec slipped off."

"Alec tried to climb onto the Black by standing on a sand dune. At first he fell off, but then he managed to stay on. The Black raced down the beach and into a ravine. When the Black slowed down, Alec was able to slip off his back."

"Alec finally managed to get onto the Black by standing on a sand dune. As soon as he got on, the Black raced off. After a wild ride, the Black slowed down and Alec was able to slip off."

If the student has difficulty with this summary, ask the following three questions to help focus his thoughts:

How did Alec get onto the Black?

Where did the Black run?

When he finally slowed down, what did Alec do?

Then have the student repeat his answers in order; this will form his brief summary. Write down the student's narration on the lines below, but do not allow him to watch.

____

____

____

____

Now ask him whether he can repeat the first sentence of the narration to himself. If not, read him the first sentence of the narration only. Tell him to listen carefully, since you will only read it once. Encourage him to repeat it to himself until he can remember it, and then to say it out loud to himself as he writes it down on Student page 279.

Give all necessary help in spelling and punctuation.

When done, set the workbook page aside for the next lesson, which is on the back of it.

Day Four: Dictation Exercise *Student page 280*

***Focus:** Contractions*

Pull out Student page 280. Ask the student to write his name and the date.

Tell the student that today's dictation sentences are also from *The Black Stallion*.

Dictate the following sentences to the student three times. Before you read, tell the student that you will read the sentences only three times before asking him to write, and will not repeat them afterwards.

Pause briefly at the comma in the last sentence. Be sure to indicate the end of each sentence by allowing your voice to fall and pausing for a longer time.

> The next day he mounted the Black again. The horse half-reared but didn't fight him. Alec spoke softly in his ear, and the Black stood still.

Now ask the student to repeat the sentences back to you before he writes. If he forgets, tell him to go back to the beginning of the sentences and recite them again to jog his memory. If necessary, you may then prompt the student with single words.

Watch the student as he writes, and correct him at once if he begins to make a mistake.

When he is finished, ask him to find and underline the contraction. He should underline the word "didn't." Ask him to write the contracted words out in full beneath his dictation. He should write "did not."

Day Five (optional): Creative Writing *Student page 281*

Pull out Student page 281. Write the student's name and the date for her as she watches, or ask her to write the name and date independently.

> **Instructor:** If you were stuck on an island with one person, who would you want it to be? What is something about that person that would make you want to have them with you on the island? If you like, draw a picture of you and your chosen friend on an island.

WEEK 31

Day One: Narration Exercise *Student pages 283–285*

***Focus:** Identifying the central narrative thread in a passage*

Pull out Student pages 283–284 and 285. Ask the student to write her name and the date on Student page 285.

Allow the student to read the story on Student pages 283–284, either silently or aloud.

You will now ask the student to summarize the passage. This selection lends itself to a narrative, story-like retelling. To guide the student towards this type of summary, ask her, "In three or four sentences, tell me about the sword in the anvil." Her answer should resemble one of the following:

> "The knights in Britain fought over who would be their leader. Then Merlin came to London and gathered all the knights together on Christmas Day. They all saw a sword in an anvil, sitting on a stone. The knights tried to pull out the sword, because the man who pulled it out would be the king of Britain, but no one could move it."

> "There was no king in Britain, so Merlin came to London and gathered the knights together. They saw a sword in an anvil with gold letters saying, 'Whoever pulls out this sword will be king of Britain.' But none of the knights could pull the sword out."

> "The men of Britain were quarrelling and the Saxons were conquering them. Britain needed a king, so Merlin made a sword in an anvil appear. The anvil was sitting on a stone that said, 'Whoso pulleth out this sword is the king of all Britain.'"

If the student has difficulty with this summary, ask the following three questions to help focus her thoughts:

> What problem did the knights of Britain have?
>
> What appeared when Merlin came to London?
>
> How did the knights react?

Write the narration down on Student page 285 as the student watches.

When done, set the workbook page aside for the next lesson, which is on the back of it.

Day Two: Dictation Exercise *Student page 286*

Focus: *Contractions*

Pull out Student page 286. Ask the student to write her name and the date.

Tell the student that contractions make a story sound modern. Read her this excerpt from a retelling of the King Arthur story by Andrew Lang, who lived over a hundred years ago (1844–1912). He writes, "When Arthur reached the house, the door was locked, and though Arthur tried his best to get in, he could not. Then he rode away in great anger and said to himself, 'Kay will not be without a sword this day. I will take that sword in the churchyard and give it to him.'"

Tell the student to repeat after you, "Though Arthur tried his best to get in, he could not." As soon as the student can repeat this sentence, ask him to contract the words "could not." He should answer "couldn't." Then have him repeat the sentence one more time, using the contraction: "Though Arthur tried his best to get in, he couldn't."

Now have the student repeat, "Kay will not be without a sword this day." As soon as he can repeat this sentence, ask him to contract the words "will not." He should answer "won't." Point out that "won't" is an irregular contraction because the *ill* actually changes to an *o.* Then have him repeat the sentence one more time, using the contraction: "Kay won't be without a sword this day."

Finally, have the student repeat, "I will take that sword in the churchyard." As soon as he can repeat this sentence, ask him to contract the words "I will." He should answer "I'll." Then have him repeat the sentence one more time, using the contraction: "I'll take that sword in the churchyard."

Tell the student you will read him the excerpt twice more. The first time you will use contractions, but the second time you will not. Tell him to listen carefully for the difference.

Read: "When Arthur reached the house, the door was locked, and though Arthur tried his best to get in, he couldn't. Then he rode away in great anger and said to himself, 'Kay won't be without a sword this day. I'll take that sword in the churchyard and give it to him.'"

Next, read: "When Arthur reached the house, the door was locked, and though Arthur tried his best to get in, he could not. Then he rode away in great anger and said to himself, 'Kay will not be without a sword this day. I will take that sword in the churchyard and give it to him.'"

Now dictate the following sentences to the student three times. Before you read, tell the student that you will read the sentences only three times before asking her to write, and will not repeat them afterwards.

> Kay won't be without a sword this day. I'll take that sword in the churchyard and give it to him.

Ask the student to repeat the sentences back to you before she writes. If she forgets, tell her to go back to the beginning of the sentences and recite them again to jog her memory. If necessary, you may then prompt the student with single words.

Watch the student as she writes, and correct her at once if she begins to make a mistake.

Day Three: Narration and Original Sentence Exercise *Student pages 287–289*

Focus: *Identifying the central narrative thread in a passage and writing original sentences*

Pull out Student pages 287–288 and 289. Ask the student to write her name and the date on Student page 289.

Today's exercise will require the student to write an original sentence. Allow the student to read the story on Student pages 287–288, either silently or aloud.

You will now ask the student to summarize the passage. This selection lends itself to a narrative, story-like retelling. To guide the student towards this type of summary, say, "In three or four sentences, tell me how Arthur pulled the sword from the anvil—both times." Her answer should resemble one of the following:

> "Arthur went to get a sword for his brother Kay. He saw the sword in the stone and pulled it out. Sir Ector told him to put it back in. Arthur put it back in and drew it back out again. Sir Ector knelt down and said that Arthur was king of the Britons."
>
> "Arthur and Kay were at the tournament, but Kay forgot his sword. Arthur rode back and pulled out the sword in the stone and brought it to Kay. When Sir Ector saw the sword, he told Arthur to put it back and then pull it out a second time."
>
> "Arthur pulled the sword out of the anvil so that Kay could use it in the tournament. When Sir Ector saw the sword, he asked Arthur how he got it. Arthur said that he pulled it from the anvil. Then he put it back into the anvil and pulled it out a second time."

If the student has difficulty with this summary, ask the following three questions to help focus her thoughts:

> Why did Arthur go get the sword in the anvil?
>
> When Sir Ector saw the sword, what did he tell Arthur to do?
>
> What did Arthur do then?

Then have the student repeat her answers in order; this will form her brief summary. Write down the student's narration on the lines below, but do not allow her to watch.

____

____

____

____

Now ask her whether she can repeat the first sentence (or first and second sentences, depending on length) of the narration to herself. If not, read her the first one or two sentences of the narration only. Tell her to listen carefully, since you will only read once. Encourage her to repeat the sentence or sentences to herself until she can remember, and then to say the words out loud to herself as she writes on Student page 289.

Give all necessary help in spelling and punctuation.

When done, set the workbook page aside for the next lesson, which is on the back of it.

Day Four: Dictation Exercise *Student page 290*

***Focus:** Memory*

Pull out Student page 290. Ask the student to write her name and the date.

Tell the student that today's dictation sentences are from T. H. White's book *The Once and Future King*, a retelling of the Arthur legends.

First, tell the student that you will read the entire description of Sir Ector's castle as she listens.

Read: "Sir Ector's castle stood in the enormous clearing in a still more enormous forest. It had a big green courtyard and a moat with pike in it. The moat was crossed by a strongly-fortified stone bridge which ended half-way across it: the other half was covered by a wooden draw-bridge which was wound up every night. As soon as you had crossed the draw-bridge you were at the top of the village street—it had only one street—and this extended for about half a mile, with little white thatched houses of mud on either side of it. The street divided the clearing into two huge fields, that on the left being cultivated in hundreds of long narrow strips, while that on the right ran down to a little river and was used as pasture. Half of the right-hand field was fenced off for hay."

Now tell the student that you will dictate the first three sentences of the paragraph to her. Tell her that this is a memory-stretcher; you don't expect her to remember the whole thing, but you would like her to write as much as she can remember before asking you to repeat.

Read the following sentences three times. Before you read, tell the student that the last sentence is divided not by a period, but by a colon. If she is not familiar with colons, write one on the bottom of Student page 290 and tell her that colons can sometimes be used in the place of periods. When you read, pause at the colon, but pause for a longer time at each period.

> Sir Ector's castle stood in the enormous clearing in a still more enormous forest. It had a big green courtyard and a moat with pike in it. The moat was crossed by a strongly-fortified stone bridge which ended half-way across it: the other half was covered by a wooden draw-bridge which was wound up every night.

Watch the student as she writes, and correct her at once if she begins to make a mistake. You will need to tell her that there is a hyphen in "strongly-fortified" and another in "half-way."

Day Five (optional): Creative Writing *Student page 291*

Pull out Student page 291. Write the student's name and the date for him as he watches, or ask him to write the name and date independently.

> **Instructor:** Would you want to be a King or Queen like Arthur, a knight like Sir Kay, or a wizard like Merlin? What is the first thing you would do in your new role? If you like, draw yourself as your chosen character.

Write the student's answer down on a separate piece of paper. First, read the sentence back to him and then have him repeat it back to you. Finally, have him write the sentence down on his own, without access to the written model. Repeat steps 1-2 if necessary until the student has written the full sentence.

WEEK 32

Day One: Narration Exercise *Student pages 293–295*

***Focus:** Identifying the central narrative thread in a passage*

Pull out Student pages 293–294 and 295. Ask the student to write his name and the date on Student page 295.

Allow the student to read the story on Student pages 293–294, either silently or aloud.

You will now ask the student to summarize the passage. This selection lends itself to a narrative, story-like retelling. To guide the student towards this type of summary, say to him, "Tell me in three sentences why the tailor wrote 'Seven in one stroke' on his belt." His answer should resemble one of the following:

> "The tailor bought some jam from a peasant woman. The flies descended on the jam, so the tailor hit them with a cloth. He killed seven flies, so he wrote 'Seven at one stroke!' on his belt."
>
> "A woman came along selling jam, and the tailor bought some. He was finishing a jacket, so he left the jam on the table. Then he killed seven of the flies that swarmed around the jam with one blow."
>
> "The little tailor bought some jam and spread it on bread. He left the bread and jam on the table, and flies swarmed all around it. The little tailor killed seven of them with a cloth, and wrote 'Seven at one stroke!' on his belt."

If the student has difficulty with this summary, ask the following three questions to help focus his thoughts:

> What did the tailor buy from the woman?
>
> What happened to the jam while it was sitting on the table?
>
> What did the tailor kill?

The answers to these questions will make up the student's summary.

Write the narration down on Student page 295 as the student watches.

When done, set the workbook page aside for the next lesson, which is on the back of it.

Day Two: Dictation Exercise *Student page 296*

***Focus:** Direct quotations at beginning, middle, and end of sentences*

> ***Note:*** Today's exercise covers direct quotations at the beginning, middle, and end of sentences. The student should have learned the rules for writing direct quotations from his grammar program. If he has not (or needs a reminder), show him the following rules and read through them with him. Ask the student to find the place where each rule is demonstrated in the dialogue.
>
> "If the direct quote is at the beginning of a sentence, it should have a comma after it," the teacher said. "The comma should go inside the closing quotation mark. The first word after the quotation should not be capitalized."
>
> "What if the quote is a question?" the student asked.
>
> "Good point!" the teacher said. "Question marks and exclamation points go inside the closing quotation mark as well. But you still shouldn't capitalize the first word after the quotation."
>
> The student said, "What if the quotation is at the end of the sentence?"
>
> The teacher said, "Then the comma should come right before the direct quotation, and the quotation should begin with a capital letter."
>
> "What if the words 'he said' come in the middle of the quotation?" the student asked.
>
> "In that case," the teacher said, "commas come after the first part of the quotation and also after the word 'said.'"

Pull out Student page 296. Ask the student to write his name and the date.

Tell the student that today's dictation sentences are from the fairy tale "Briar Rose," another story collected by the Brothers Grimm. He may know it by the name "Sleeping Beauty."

Before you dictate, read the first paragraph of the story to the student: "A king and queen once upon a time reigned in a country a great way off, where there were in those days fairies. Now this king and queen had plenty of money, and plenty of fine clothes to wear, and plenty of good things to eat and drink, and a coach to ride out in every day: but though they had been married many years they had no children, and this grieved them very much indeed. But one day as the queen was walking by the side of the river, at the bottom of the garden, she saw a poor little fish, that had thrown itself out of the water, and lay gasping and nearly dead on the bank. Then the queen took pity on the little fish, and threw it back again into the river."

Now dictate the following sentences to the student three times. Before you read, tell the student that you will read the sentences only three times before asking him to write, and will not repeat them afterwards. Also tell him that there is a direct quote in the selection. Remind him that a direct quote should have quotation marks around it, and that it should be separated from the sentence before it by a comma. Be sure to use a different voice for the fish's exact words.

> Before the little fish swam away, it lifted its head out of the water and said, "I know what your wish is, and it shall be fulfilled, in return for your kindness to me. You will soon have a daughter."

Now ask the student to repeat the sentences back to you before he writes. If he forgets, tell him to go back to the beginning of the sentences and recite them again to jog his memory. If necessary, you may then prompt the student with single words.

Watch the student as he writes, and correct him at once if he begins to make a mistake. If he writes "it's" instead of "its," remind him that "its" is the possessive form of "it," while "it's" is a contraction for "it is" ("it lifted it is head out of the water" wouldn't make any sense!).

Day Three: Narration and Original Sentence Exercise *Student pages 297–299*

Focus: *Identifying the central narrative thread in a passage and writing original sentences*

Pull out Student pages 297–298 and 299. Ask the student to write his name and the date on Student page 299.

Today's exercise will require the student to write an original sentence. Allow the student to read the story on Student pages 297–298, either silently or aloud.

You will now ask the student to summarize the passage. This selection lends itself to a narrative, story-like retelling. To guide the student towards this type of summary, say to him, "Tell me the three things that the tailor did to impress the giant." (Do not give him a sentence limit.) His answer should resemble one of the following:

> "First, the tailor squeezed the liquid out of a cheese, and the giant thought he was squeezing a rock. Then, the tailor threw a bird into the air, and the giant thought he was throwing a stone. Then the tailor told the giant he would carry the branches of a tree, but instead he rode on it while the giant carried it."
>
> "The giant squeezed a rock until water ran out, and the tailor did the same thing with a piece of cheese. Next the giant threw a rock into the air. The tailor threw a bird, which flew up out of sight. Then the giant told the tailor to carry a tree. Instead, the tailor let the giant carry it while he rode in the branches."
>
> "When the giant told the tailor to squeeze water out of a rock, the tailor squeezed water out of a cheese. The giant threw a rock high into the air and told the tailor to do the same. The tailor threw a bird into the air, and the bird did not come back. Then the giant told the tailor to help carry a tree. The tailor said that he would carry the branches, but he let the giant do all the work while he rode on the tree."

If the student has difficulty with this summary, ask the following three questions to help focus his thoughts:

Why did the tailor squeeze the cheese?

Why did the tailor throw the bird into the air?

Why did the tailor ride in the branches of the tree?

Then have the student repeat his answers in order; this will form his brief summary. Write down the student's narration on the lines below, but do not allow him to watch.

____

____

____

____

Now ask him whether he can repeat the first sentence (or first and second sentences, depending on length) of the narration to himself. If not, read him the first one or two sentences of the narration only. Tell him to listen carefully, since you will only read once. Encourage him to repeat the sentence or sentences to himself until he can remember, and then to say the words out loud to himself as he writes on Student page 299.

Give all necessary help in spelling and punctuation.

When done, set the workbook page aside for the next lesson, which is on the back of it.

Day Four: Dictation Exercise *Student page 300*

Focus: *Direct quotations at beginning, middle, and end of sentences*

Pull out Student page 300. Ask the student to write his name and the date.

Tell the student that today's dictation sentences are also from the fairy tale "Briar Rose." Read the following paragraphs of the story to the student:

> The queen had a little girl, so very beautiful that the king said he would hold a great feast and make merry, and show the child to all the land. So he asked his kinsmen, and nobles, and friends, and neighbours. But the queen said, "I will have the fairies also, that they might be kind and good to our little daughter." Now there were thirteen fairies in the kingdom; but as the king and queen had only twelve golden dishes for them to eat out of, they were forced to leave one of the fairies without asking her. So twelve fairies came, and after the feast was over they gathered round in a ring and gave all their best gifts to the little princess. One gave her goodness, another beauty, another riches, and so on till she had all that was good in the world.

Just as eleven of them had done blessing her, a great noise was heard in the courtyard, and word was brought that the thirteenth fairy was come. Now, as she had not been asked to the feast she was very angry, and scolded the king and queen very much, and set to work to take her revenge. So she cried out, "The king's daughter shall, in her fifteenth year, be wounded by a spindle, and fall down dead." Then the twelfth of the friendly fairies, who had not yet given her gift, came forward, and said that the evil wish must be fulfilled, but that she could soften its mischief; so her gift was, that the king's daughter, when the spindle wounded her, should not really die, but should only fall asleep for a hundred years.

However, the king hoped still to save his dear child altogether from the threatened evil; so he ordered that all the spindles in the kingdom should be bought up and burnt. But all the gifts of the first eleven fairies were in the meantime fulfilled; for the princess was so beautiful, and well behaved, and good, and wise, that everyone who knew her loved her.

It happened that, on the very day she was fifteen years old, the king and queen were not at home, and she was left alone in the palace. So she roved about by herself, and looked at all the rooms and chambers, till at last she came to an old tower, to which there was a narrow staircase ending with a little door. In the door there was a golden key, and when she turned it the door sprang open, and there sat an old lady spinning away very busily.

Tell the student that the next two sentences of the story are today's dictation exercise. Dictate the following sentences to the student three times. Before you read, tell the student that you will read the sentences four times before asking him to write, since he will need to remember several different types of punctuation as he writes.

Be sure to use different voices for the princess and the old lady. Indicate the question at the end of the first sentence with your voice. Pause briefly at each comma.

"Why, good mother," said the princess, "what are you doing there?"
"Spinning," said the old lady, and nodded her head, humming a tune.

Now ask the student to repeat the sentences back to you before he writes. If he forgets, tell him to go back to the beginning of the sentences and recite them again to jog his memory. If necessary, you may then prompt the student with single words.

Remind the student that there should be commas between each speech and the words "said" in each sentence. Also remind him that in the first sentence, the word "what" should not be capitalized because it is part of the same sentence as "Why, good mother."

Watch the student as he writes on Student page 300, and correct him at once if he begins to make a mistake. You will probably need to tell him to begin a new paragraph with the second speech.

When the student is finished writing, tell him that when an author writes a story, he usually begins a new paragraph whenever a new speaker begins to talk.

Day Five (optional): Creative Writing *Student page 301*

Pull out Student page 301. Write the student's name and the date for her as she watches, or ask her to write the name and date independently.

> **Instructor:** The tailor became famous after killing seven flies with one blow. Tell me about a time when you did something that you were proud of or tried something even though it was scary. If you like, draw an illustration to go with your story.

WEEK 33

Day One: Narration Exercise *Student pages 303–305*

***Focus:** Identifying the central details in a passage*

Pull out Student pages 303–304 and 305. Ask the student to write her name and the date on Student page 305.

Allow the student to read the story on Student pages 303–304, either silently or aloud.

You will now ask the student to summarize the passage. A detail-oriented summary is more appropriate to this descriptive passage than a summary telling what happens. Say to the student, "In three or four sentences, describe four things that Bambi saw in the meadow." Her answer should resemble one of the following:

> "The meadow was filled with white daisies, red and purple clover, and golden dandelions. Bambi saw butterflies that looked like flying flowers. When he looked down at the ground, he saw ants running in swarms and a grasshopper jumping."
>
> "Bambi saw the meadow covered with green grass and beautiful flowers. Butterflies were fluttering above the grass. A swarm of ants ran under his hooves. A grasshopper jumped up in front of Bambi, and Bambi thought he was a piece of grass."
>
> "The green meadow was filled with white daisies and golden dandelions. Butterflies flew above the grass like flying flowers. Bambi saw ants beneath his hoofs and a grasshopper leaping in front of him."

If the student has trouble choosing important details, give her these three pointers:

> Describe the meadow and the flowers.
>
> Tell me about the butterflies.
>
> Describe the two kinds of insects that Bambi saw.

The answers to these questions will make up the student's summary.

Write the narration down on Student page 305 as the student watches.

When done, set the workbook page aside for the next lesson, which is on the back of it.

Day Two: Dictation Exercise *Student page 306*

***Focus:** Direct quotations at beginning, middle, and end of sentences*

Pull out Student page 306. Ask the student to write her name and the date.

Tell the student that today's dictation sentences are also from the book *Bambi.* Before you dictate, read the following dialogue to the student. Tell her that Bambi and his mother have this conversation while walking in the woods.

> Once he asked, "Whom does this trail belong to, Mother?"
> His mother answered, "To us."
> Bambi asked again, "To you and me?"
> "Yes."
> "To us two?"
> "Yes."
> "Only to us two?"
> "No," said his mother, "to us deer."
> "What are deer?" Bambi asked, and laughed.
> His mother looked at him from head to foot and laughed too. "You are a deer and I am a deer. We're both deer," she said. "Do you understand?"

Now dictate the following sentences to the student three times. Before you read, tell the student that you will read the sentences only three times before asking her to write, and will not repeat them afterwards.

Be sure to use a different voice for the mother's voice. Indicate the periods by pausing and allowing your voice to fall; remember to indicate the question mark by using a questioning voice for the last phrase.

> His mother looked at him from head to foot and laughed too. "You are a deer and I am a deer. We're both deer," she said. "Do you understand?"

Now ask the student to repeat the sentences back to you before she writes. If she forgets, tell her to go back to the beginning of the sentences and recite them again to jog her memory. If necessary, you may then prompt the student with single words.

Watch the student as she writes on Student page 306. Correct her at once if she begins to make a mistake.

Day Three: Narration and Original Sentence Exercise *Student pages 307–309*

***Focus:** Identifying the central details in a passage and writing original sentences*

Pull out Student pages 307–308 and 309. Ask the student to write her name and the date on Student page 309.

Today's exercise will require the student to write an original sentence. Allow the student to read the story on Student pages 307–308, either silently or aloud.

You will now ask the student to summarize the passage. A detail-oriented summary is more appropriate to this descriptive passage than a summary telling what happens. Say to the student, "In three or four sentences, describe Bambi's meeting with the Hare." Her answer should resemble one of the following:

> "Bambi saw his mother standing still, and he went over to see what she was doing. She was talking to the Hare. He had tall spoonlike ears with black stripes, stiff whiskers, and big round eyes. Bambi did not feel any respect for the Hare."

"Bambi saw the Hare's two long ears in the grass. The Hare had a mild face, good-natured features, and big round eyes. His mouth and nose twitched, and Bambi had to laugh at him."

"The Hare had spoonlike, grayish-brown ears with black stripes. The Hare was polite and mild, and Bambi did not feel any respect for him. The Hare sat up suddenly with his nose twitching and then hopped quickly away."

If the student has difficulty with this summary, ask the following three questions to help focus her thoughts:

What did Bambi see when he went over to his mother?

Can you describe the Hare's ears and face?

How did Bambi feel towards the Hare?

Then have the student repeat her answers in order; this will form her brief summary. Write down the student's narration on the lines below, but do not allow her to watch.

____

____

____

____

Now ask her whether she can repeat the first sentence (or first and second sentences, depending on length) of the narration to herself. If not, read her the first one or two sentences of the narration only. Tell her to listen carefully, since you will only read once. Encourage her to repeat the sentence or sentences to herself until she can remember, and then to say the words out loud to herself as she writes on Student page 309.

Give all necessary help in spelling and punctuation.

When done, set the workbook page aside for the next lesson, which is on the back of it.

Day Four: Dictation Exercise — *Student page 310*

Focus: *Direct quotations at beginning, middle, and end of sentences*

Pull out Student page 310. Ask the student to write her name and the date.

Tell the student that today's dictation sentences are also from the book *Bambi.* Before you dictate, read the following paragraph to the student. It describes how Bambi develops the ability to smell what is going on in the woods.

> He knew how to snuff the air now, too. Soon he would do it as well as his mother. He could breathe in the air and at the same time analyze it with his senses. "That's clover and meadow grass," he would think when the wind blew off the fields. "And Friend Hare is out there, too. I can smell him plainly."

Now dictate the following sentences to the student three times. Before you read, tell the student that you will read the sentences only three times before asking her to write, and will not repeat them afterwards.

Use a different voice for Bambi's thoughts. Be sure to indicate the periods by allowing your voice to fall. Pause briefly at the comma in the second sentence. Before the student writes, tell her that "Friend Hare" is capitalized because Bambi is using it as a proper name.

> "That's clover and meadow grass," he would think when the wind blew off the fields. "And Friend Hare is out there, too. I can smell him plainly."

Now ask the student to repeat the sentences back to you before she writes. If she forgets, tell her to go back to the beginning of the sentences and recite them again to jog her memory. If necessary, you may then prompt the student with single words.

Watch the student as she writes on Student page 310. Correct her at once if she begins to make a mistake. You may need to remind her to use an apostrophe in "that's" because it is a contraction of "that is."

Day Five (optional): Creative Writing *Student page 311*

Pull out Student page 311. Write the student's name and the date for him as he watches, or ask him to write the name and date independently.

> **Instructor:** Imagine you could become any animal that lives in the forest. Which animal would you want to be? Why? OR Imagine you are a rabbit that lives in the forest. Tell me about your day? How would you spend your time? If you like, draw a picture of the forest.

WEEK 34

Day One: Narration Exercise *Student pages 313–315*

Focus: *Identifying the central narrative thread in a passage*

Pull out Student pages 313–314 and 315. Ask the student to write his name and the date on Student page 315.

Allow the student to read the story on Student pages 313–314, either silently or aloud.

You will now ask the student to summarize the passage. This selection lends itself to a narrative, story-like retelling. To guide the student towards this type of summary, ask him, "Tell me what happened to Prince Wicked and the three animals. Be sure to include how the animals and the prince felt towards the poor man after they were rescued." He should take five or six sentences for his answer, which should resemble one of the following:

> "Prince Wicked was swept into the river. He climbed onto a log. A rat, a snake, and a parrot were also forced to climb onto the log. A poor man rescued them and took care of the animals first. The animals were grateful to him, but the prince secretly hated him."
>
> "Prince Wicked was so wicked that his servants left him to drown. He climbed onto a log and floated down the river. A rat and a snake were also swept into the river and climbed onto the log. Then a parrot was forced to land on it. They were all rescued by a poor man. The animals thanked the poor man, but the prince hated him because the poor man took care of the animals first."
>
> "Prince Wicked fell into the river and floated down it on a log. A rat, a snake, and a parrot also climbed onto the log for safety. A poor man rescued all of them and took care of the animals first, because they were weaker. The snake promised him gold, the rat promised him money, and the parrot promised him rice. But the prince hated him."

If the student has difficulty condensing this story into a summary, ask the following four questions to help focus his thoughts:

> What happened to Prince Wicked at the beginning of the story?
>
> What three animals joined him?
>
> When they were rescued, how were the animals treated differently?
>
> How did the animals and the prince feel towards the poor man?

The answers to these questions will make up the student's summary.

Write the narration down on Student page 315 as the student watches.

When done, set the workbook page aside for the next lesson, which is on the back of it.

Day Two: Dictation Exercise *Student page 316*

Focus: *Comparative and superlative adjectives*

Pull out Student page 316. Ask the student to write his name and the date.

Tell the student that today's dictation sentence is from another of the Jataka tales retold by Ellen Babbitt. The tale is called "The Wise Goat and the Wolf."

Before you dictate, read the beginning paragraph to the student: "Once upon a time, many, many wild goats lived in a cave in the side of a hill. A wolf lived with his mate not far from this cave. Like all wolves they liked the taste of goat. So they caught the goats, one after another, and ate them all but one who was wiser than all the others. Try as they might the wolves could not catch her."

Now dictate the following sentences to the student three times. Before you read, tell the student that you will read the sentences only three times before asking him to write, and will not repeat them afterwards.

> Like all wolves they liked the taste of goat. So they caught the goats, one after another, and ate them all but one who was wiser than all the others.

Now ask the student to repeat the sentences back to you before he writes. If he forgets, tell him to go back to the beginning of the sentences and recite them again to jog his memory. If necessary, you may then prompt the student with single words.

Watch the student as he writes, and correct him at once if he begins to make a mistake.

When the student is finished, ask him to underline the word "wiser" in the second sentence. Tell him that this is a *comparative adjective*. Most adjectives have three forms: the regular form, the comparative form, and the superlative form. The regular form of this adjective is "wise." All of the goats might be wise. The comparative form is "wiser." One goat is "wiser" than the rest. Can the student guess the superlative form? It is "wisest." Maybe this goat is the "wisest" of all the goats in the world!

Day Three: Narration and Original Sentence Exercise *Student pages 317–319*

Focus: *Identifying the central narrative thread in a passage and writing original sentences*

Pull out Student pages 317–318 and 319. Ask the student to write his name and the date on Student page 319.

Today's exercise will require the student to write an original sentence. Allow the student to read the story on Student pages 317–318, either silently or aloud.

You will now ask the student to summarize the passage. This selection lends itself to a narrative, story-like retelling. To guide the student towards this type of summary, say to him, "Tell me about the poor man and the animals. Then tell me about the poor man and Prince

Wicked." His answer should be five or six sentences long and should resemble one of the following:

> "The poor man went to see each one of the animals to see if they would keep their promises. All of them did. Then the poor man went to see the prince. The prince was now the king. He ordered the poor man beaten and put to death. But the people killed the king instead and made the poor man king in his place."
>
> "The snake showed the poor man where the gold was. The rat showed him where money was buried. The parrot said that he and his family and friends would gather rice. But the prince, who was now king, was afraid that he would have to give the poor man riches. He ordered the poor man put to death. Instead, the people made the poor man king in his place."
>
> "The snake, the rat, and the parrot all kept their promises. So the poor man went to the city to see Prince Wicked, who was now the king. The king didn't want to keep his promise, so he told his servants to arrest and beat the poor man. The poor man told his story to some wise men in the city. The wise men and the rest of the people killed the wicked king and made the poor man king instead."

If the student has difficulty with this summary, ask the following four questions to help focus his thoughts:

> What did the three animals do when the poor man went to see them?
>
> What had happened to the prince in the meantime?
>
> When the king saw the poor man, what did he tell his servants to do?
>
> How did the people of the city react to this?

Then have the student repeat his answers in order; this will form his brief summary. Write down the student's narration on the lines below, but do not allow him to watch.

____

____

____

____

Now ask him whether he can repeat the first sentence (or first and second sentences, depending on length) of the narration to himself. If not, read him the first one or two sentences of the narration only. Tell him to listen carefully, since you will only read once. Encourage him to repeat the sentence or sentences to himself until he can remember, and then to say the words out loud to himself as he writes on Student page 319.

Give all necessary help in spelling and punctuation.

When done, set the workbook page aside for the next lesson, which is on the back of it.

Day Four: Dictation Exercise *Student page 320*

***Focus:** Comparative and superlative adjectives*

Pull out Student page 320. Ask the student to write his name and the date.

Tell the student that today's dictation sentence is from another of the Jataka tales retold by Ellen Babbitt. It is called "The Quarrel of the Quails." Before you dictate, read the first paragraphs of the story to the student:

> Once upon a time many quails lived together in a forest. The wisest of them all was their leader.
>
> A man lived near the forest and earned his living by catching quails and selling them. Day after day he listened to the note of the leader calling the quails. By and by this man, the fowler, was able to call the quails together. Hearing the note the quails thought it was their leader who called.
>
> When they were crowded together, the fowler threw the net over them and off he went into the town, where he soon sold all the quails that he had caught.

Tell the student that the leader of the quails thought of a plan to escape from the fowler, but he'll have to find the story and read it to find out what the plan was.

Now dictate the following sentences to the student three times. Before you read, tell the student that you will read the sentences only three times before asking him to write, and will not repeat them afterwards.

> Once upon a time many quails lived together in a forest. The wisest of them all was their leader.

Now ask the student to repeat the sentences back to you before he writes. If he forgets, tell him to go back to the beginning of the sentences and recite them again to jog his memory. If necessary, you may then prompt the student with single words.

Watch the student as he writes on Student page 320. Correct him at once if he begins to make a mistake.

When the student is finished, ask him to underline the word "wisest" in the second sentence. Ask him if he remembers what form of the adjective "wise" this is. The correct answer is the "superlative" form. Remind him that most adjectives have three forms: the regular form, the comparative form, and the superlative form. The regular form of this adjective is "wise." All of the quails might be wise. The comparative form is "wiser." Some of the quails might be "wiser" than the others. The superlative form is "wisest." The leader of the quails is the "wisest" of them all.

Day Five (optional): Creative Writing *Student page 321*

Pull out Student page 321. Write the student's name and the date for her as she watches, or ask her to write the name and date independently.

> **Instructor:** In the story, Prince Wicked has no gratitude for the old man who saved his life. Write down a list of two or three things you are grateful for. If you like, draw a picture of yourself smiling.

WEEK 35

Day One: Narration Exercise *Student pages 323–325*

***Focus:** Identifying the central narrative thread in a passage, along with relevant details*

Pull out Student pages 323–324 and 325. Ask the student to write her name and the date on Student page 325.

Allow the student to read the story on Student pages 323–324, either silently or aloud.

You will now ask the student to summarize the passage. This passage has a strong narrative thread, but it also contains important details. To help the student in summarizing, say, "Give me two sentences telling what the Monkey People are like, and then two sentences telling what they do to Mowgli." Her answer should resemble one of the following:

> "The Monkey People lived in the treetops and threw sticks and nuts at other animals. They had no leader or laws or customs of their own. They decided to kidnap Mowgli because he could help them make houses to live in. So they grabbed Mowgli during his nap and dragged him away through the treetops."

> "The Monkey People lived in the trees, and none of the other animals would notice them. They howled and shrieked and started fights over nothing. They kidnapped Mowgli while he was sleeping and carried him away through the treetops. Mowgli enjoyed rushing through the branches, even though it frightened him."

> "The Monkey People lived in the trees and had their own roads and crossroads in the treetops. They always intended to have leaders and laws, but they could never remember this the next day. When they saw Mowgli making play huts, they decided that he could live with them and be their leader. They snatched him away from Baloo and Bagheera and carried him off through the treetops."

If the student has difficulty condensing the selection, ask these four questions:

Where did the monkeys live?

Why didn't they have leaders and laws?

Why did they decide to kidnap Mowgli?

How did they get him away from Baloo and Bagheera?

The answers to these questions will make up the student's summary.

Write the narration down on Student page 325 as the student watches.

When done, set the workbook page aside for the next lesson, which is on the back of it.

Day Two: Dictation Exercise *Student page 326*

***Focus:** Interjections*

Pull out Student page 326. Ask the student to write her name and the date.

Tell the student that today's dictation sentences are from Rudyard Kipling's story "Rikki-tikki-tavi," found in *The Jungle Book*. Rikki-tikki is a mongoose who lives with a British family in India. His instinct is to kill snakes, so when he finds two cobras living in the garden, he tries to get rid of them. The following sentence tells what happens when Rikki-tikki destroys all of the cobra's eggs except for one.

Dictate the following sentences to the student three times. Before you read, tell the student that you will read the sentences only three times before asking her to write, and will not repeat them afterwards.

Also tell the student that "Ah!" is spelled *ah* and should be followed by an exclamation point. Be sure to use a different voice for the snake's words. Pause briefly at the comma in the first sentence. Pause for a longer time at the period, and indicate the end of the sentence by allowing your voice to fall.

> The big snake turned half round, and saw the egg on the veranda. "Ah! Give it to me," she said.

Now ask the student to repeat the sentences back to you before she writes. If she forgets, tell her to go back to the beginning of the sentences and recite them again to jog her memory. If necessary, you may then prompt the student with single words.

Watch the student as she writes, and correct her at once if she begins to make a mistake.

When the student is finished writing, ask her to underline the word "Ah!" Tell her that this is an *interjection*. An interjection shows emotion and doesn't have any grammatical relationship to the rest of the sentence. It can be in a sentence all by itself, like "Ah!"

Day Three: Narration and Original Sentence Exercise *Student pages 327–329*

***Focus:** Identifying the central details in a passage and writing original sentences*

Pull out Student pages 327–328 and 329. Ask the student to write her name and the date on Student page 329.

Today's exercise will require the student to write an original sentence. Allow the student to read the story on Student pages 327–328, either silently or aloud.

You will now ask the student to summarize the passage. A detail-oriented summary is more appropriate to this descriptive passage than a summary telling what happens. Say to the student, "Give me two sentences describing the Lost City, and two sentences describing what the monkeys did there." Her answer should resemble one of the following:

> "The Lost City had trees and creepers growing through it. The palace had no roof, and rows and rows of houses with no roofs lined the streets. The monkeys pretended that they were men and used the council chamber. They explored the city, but they could never remember what they saw."
>
> "The gates of the Lost City were ruined and the battlements had fallen down. The domes of the temples were shattered and the houses had no roofs. The monkeys lived in the city and pretended to be men, but they didn't know what the buildings were for. They played in the garden, explored the tunnels, and drank from the tanks."
>
> "The monkeys called the Lost City their city, but they didn't know what the buildings were for. The city was ruined; the palace on the hill had no roof, and trees and vines grew everywhere. Rows and rows of roofless houses made up the rest of the city. The monkeys collected bits of brick and plaster, fought with each other, and pretended to be men."

If the student has difficulty with this summary, ask the following three questions to help focus her thoughts:

> Describe the palace in the Lost City.
>
> Describe something else seen in the streets of the Lost City.
>
> Now tell me what the monkeys pretended to be, and how.

Then have the student repeat her answers in order; this will form her brief summary. Write down the student's narration on the lines below, but do not allow her to watch.

____

____

____

____

Now ask her whether she can repeat the first sentence (or first and second sentences, depending on length) of the narration to herself. If not, read her the first one or two sentences of the narration only. Tell her to listen carefully, since you will only read once. Encourage her to repeat the sentence or sentences to herself until she can remember, and then to say the words out loud to herself as she writes on Student page 329.

Give all necessary help in spelling and punctuation.

When done, set the workbook page aside for the next lesson, which is on the back of it.

Day Four: Dictation Exercise *Student page 330*

Focus: *Interjections*

Pull out Student page 330. Ask the student to write her name and the date.

Tell the student that today's dictation sentences are also from Rudyard Kipling's story "Rikki-tikki-tavi," found in *The Jungle Book*. In this selection, Rikki-tikki is startled by the mother and father of the family, who have come into the room where he is sleeping.

Begin by reading the following two paragraphs to the student:

> "Oh, it's you," said he. "What are you bothering for? All the cobras are dead; and if they weren't, I'm here."
>
> Rikki-tikki had a right to be proud of himself; but he did not grow too proud, and he kept that garden as a mongoose should keep it, with tooth and jump and spring and bite, till never a cobra dared show its head inside the walls.

Now dictate the following sentences to the student three times. Before you read, tell the student that you will read the sentences only three times before asking her to write, and will not repeat them afterwards.

Be sure to indicate the commas by pausing slightly. Indicate the question by allowing your voice to rise. Before you read, tell the student that there is a semicolon in the selection. The semicolon will be a longer pause than a comma, but a shorter pause than a period, and it will separate two complete sentences. Tell the student to listen carefully for the semicolon.

> "Oh, it's you," said he. "What are you bothering for? All the cobras are dead; and if they weren't, I'm here."

Now ask the student to repeat the sentences back to you before she writes. If she forgets, tell her to go back to the beginning of the sentences and recite them again to jog her memory. If necessary, you may then prompt the student with single words.

Watch the student as she writes, and correct her at once if she begins to make a mistake. You may need to remind her that "it's" is the contraction of "it is" and has an apostrophe.

When the student is finished writing, ask her to underline the word "Oh." Tell her that this is another *interjection*. An interjection can be in a sentence all by itself—like "Ah!"—but it can also be connected to another sentence with a comma.

Day Five (optional): Creative Writing *Student page 331*

Pull out Student page 331. Write the student's name and the date for him as he watches, or ask him to write the name and date independently.

Instructor: If you were exploring the jungle with Mowgli, what are three animals you might find? Describe at least one of the animals using comparative and superlative adjectives. If you like, draw a picture of the jungle.

Note To Instructor: If your student needs help, provide them with some sample adjectives they could use: big, bigger, biggest, fast, faster, fastest, small, smaller, smallest, or scary, scarier, scariest.

WEEK 36: EVALUATION

Before moving to Level Four, the student should be able to read a passage independently and sum it up in two to six sentences (depending on length). He should be able to write down at least the first sentence of his own narration. He should also be able to take down dictation exercises of two to three sentences after three repetitions.

Use the following assignments to evaluate the student's mastery of these skills; you may do these over several days or all at once, depending on the student's maturity.

If the student still struggles with narration or dictation skills, spend a few more weeks on these skills before moving on.

Narration and Original Sentence Evaluation *Evaluation Pages 1–3*

Pull out Evaluation Pages 1–3. Ask the student to write his name and the date on Evaluation Page 3.

Give Evaluation Pages 1–2 to the student to read independently.

When he is finished reading, ask him to summarize the passage in three sentences. His answer should resemble one of the following:

> "Little Georgie ran away from the Old Hound, so fast that it felt like flying. But when he came over a hill, he saw Deadman's Brook in front of him. He leaped all the way over the brook, and the Old Hound gave up and went slowly home."
>
> "The Old Hound was chasing Little Georgie, and Little Georgie could not find anywhere to hide. He wondered why the Old Hound didn't give up, until he came to Deadman's Brook. He had to jump over it, even though he was frightened."
>
> "Little George was running away from the Old Hound when he saw a stream in front of him. It was so wide that he didn't think he could jump across it. But he leaped as hard as he could, sailed across, and landed safely on the other side."

Write down the student's narration on the lines below, but do not allow him to watch.

____

____

____

____

Now ask him to repeat the first sentence of the narration to himself. If he cannot remember it, read him the first sentence of the narration ONLY ONCE. Tell the student to repeat the sentence to himself, and then to say it out loud to himself as he writes it down on Evaluation Page 3.

Give all necessary help in spelling and punctuation.

When done, set the workbook page aside for the next lesson, which is on the back of it.

DICTATION EVALUATION *Evaluation Page 4*

Pull out Evaluation Page 4. Ask the student to write his name and the date.

Tell the student that today's dictation sentences are from *Rabbit Hill.* Before Georgie sets off on his journey, his father wants to make sure that he knows how to cross over a bridge safely. He asks Georgie, "What do you do when you come to a bridge?" This is Georgie's response.

Dictate the following sentences to the student three times. Before you read, tell the student that you will read the sentences only three times before asking him to write, and will not repeat them afterwards. Be sure to indicate the periods and commas with appropriate pauses. Use inflection to indicate the ends of sentences, and use a different voice for Georgie's exact words.

> "I hide well," answered Georgie, "and wait a good long time. I look all around for dogs. I look up the road for cars and down the road for cars."

Now ask the student to repeat the sentences back to you before he writes. He should not need you to prompt him with single words.

Allow the student to write without interruption. You may help him spell "Georgie," but he should not need any other assistance with spelling or punctuation.

WRITING WITH EASE AND *WRITING WITH SKILL*: SUSAN'S UPDATED RECOMMENDATIONS

In 2008, Well-Trained Mind Press began publishing *Writing With Ease,* which fleshes the general elementary writing recommendations in *The Well-Trained Mind* out into a full curriculum. *Writing With Skill,* which does the same for the logic stage (pre-rhetoric recommendations), followed.

We've been fortunate that many thousands of parents have made use of these programs—and have given us plenty of feedback about their experience. Here are three things I've learned . . .

You'll Probably Need to Repeat the Dictations More than Three Times

Throughout Writing With Ease, I suggest that you repeat dictation sentences three times. If a student can hold the dictations in his head after three repetitions, that's great. Ideal, in fact.

But as we all know, "ideal" isn't "real." Many students need additional repetitions. And as you get into the more complex dictations, *most* students will need you to say the dictation sentences additional times.

That's absolutely fine. Don't frustrate your young writer. Repeat the sentences again.

And, if necessary, again. And again. BUT, follow these two rules:

1) Always ask the student to repeat the sentence back to you before she goes back to writing.

2) Always repeat the dictation assignment from the beginning. Don't allow the student to write one word at time as you "feed" the sentence to her.

Three Levels of *Writing With Ease* is Enough

The purpose of the readings, narrations, and dictations in *Writing With Ease* is to develop critical skills in writing—putting ideas into words, getting words down on paper, and holding words in your head long enough to write them out. (If you're not familiar with the need for these skills, be sure to read my short essay "Why Writing Programs Fail," which can be found on the Well-Trained Mind website.)

For most students, those skills are in place by the end of *Writing With Ease, Level Three.*

In fact, many students who are perfectly ready to go on to original writing (the next step in the process) are frustrated by the more complex sentences in our original Level Four—particularly the dictation exercises.

So we suggest that you complete *Writing With Ease* 1-3, and then follow one of the options in the chart below, keeping this last point in mind . . .

Fifth Grade is Generally Too Early for *Writing With Skill*

Writing With Skill is one very specific, parts-to-whole, step-by-step outworking of the principles laid out in my writing workshops (available as audio downloads on the Well-Trained Mind website). It is a *pre-rhetoric* course, designed to give students the skills necessary to 1) compose well-organized, properly researched and documented short pieces of expository writing across the curriculum, and 2) prepare them to go into a high school or freshman college rhetoric course.

So, although it is the next logical step after *Writing With Ease* in the student's writing development, it doesn't necessarily have to be completed *immediately* after the *Writing With Ease* series. In fact, most students seem to benefit from a year or more of writing across the curriculum or using another writing program. This additional maturity reduces frustration levels, makes the texts used in *Writing With Skill* more accessible, and still gets the student ready for rhetoric in plenty of time.

Here are a few possible scenarios that you might follow...all of them completely compatible with the writing goals I discuss in my workshops. (Please note that I'm not necessarily making full endorsements and recommendations of the listed curricula—simply trying to give you a sense of how a number of different progressions can get a student to high school rhetoric in time.)

GRADE	First Scenario	Second Scenario	Third Scenario	Fourth Scenario
First	Writing With Ease 1	Writing With Ease 1		
Second	Writing With Ease 2	Writing With Ease 2	Writing With Ease 1	Writing With Ease 1
Third	Writing With Ease 3	Writing With Ease 3	Writing With Ease 2	Writing With Ease 2
Fourth	Continue narrations and summaries across the curriculum	Killgallon, Sentence Composing for Middle School	Writing With Ease 3	Writing With Ease 3
Fifth	Continue narrations and summaries across the curriculum	Killgallon, Paragraph Composing for Middle School	Writing With Skill 1, half speed	Bravewriter course
Sixth	Writing With Skill 1	Killgallon, Sentence Composing for High School	Writing With Skill 1, half speed	Bravewriter course
Seventh	Writing With Skill 2	Writing With Skill 1	Writing With Skill 2, half speed	Follow TWTM recommendations for outlining, summarizing, etc.
Eighth	Writing With Skill 3	Writing With Skill 2	Writing With Skill 2, half speed	Writing With Skill 1
Ninth	Continue to write short researched compositions across the curriculum	Writing With Skill 3	Writing With Skill 3	Writing With Skill 2

GRADE	First Scenario	Second Scenario	Third Scenario	Fourth Scenario
Tenth	Gerald Graff and Cathy Birkenstein, *They Say, I Say: The Moves that Matter in Academic Writing* and *Schaum's Quick Guide to Writing Great Research Papers*, plus regular persuasive papers across the curriculum	Well-Trained Mind Academy Rhetoric 1	Classical Academic Press, Writing & Rhetoric, Books 7, 8, 9	Writing With Skill 3
Eleventh	Frank D'Angelo, *Composition in the Classical Tradition,* plus regular persuasive papers across the curriculum	Well-Trained Mind Academy Rhetoric 2	Classical Academic Press, Writing & Rhetoric, Books 10, 11, 12	Well-Trained Mind Academy Rhetoric 1
Twelfth	Thomas Kane, *The New Oxford Guide to Writing* plus regular persuasive papers across the curriculum	Advanced writing or literature elective	Thomas Kane, *The New Oxford Guide to Writing* plus regular persuasive papers across the curriculum	Well-Trained Mind Academy Rhetoric 2